BREAKING UP

— WITH —

ANXIETY

A Journey to Reclaim My Life

WHITNEY ROSE

Cover Design by 100Covers.com
Interior Design by FormattedBooks.com

ISBN 978-0-578-66867-3

In memory and honor of my **Dad,**
who taught me to be a warrior
and never give up.

INTRODUCTION

It is just days before my thirty-fourth birthday. Thirty-four trips around the sun. Thirty-four years of anxiety. Thirty-four years of smiles, laughs, love, joy, adventure, experience, learning, and growing. But mostly, anxiety.

From the first moments that I can remember, I was anxious. People would often say, "She's just shy. One day she will come out of her shell." Or, as my father used to say, "She just needs to 'get over it' and then she'll be unstoppable."

Growing up, there was no trauma in my childhood. There were no extenuating circumstances that would lead doctors to believe I had an anxiety disorder. I had two amazing parents, Barry and Susan, who were happily married. My father was a successful, seasoned businessman, who often traveled for work. My mother had been an animation and illustration artist before having children. When we were young, she stayed home with us and decided to go back to work in retail when we were a little older. I was the middle child of three children, each born in the summertime, three years apart from each other. We lived in a safe, upper-middle-class small town in the suburbs of Boston, MA. I was raised in a happy, loving, and deeply spiritual family.

One of the biggest saving graces in my life was being brought up in a spiritual household. My parents started meditating in 1971 when they were twenty-one years old. Their practice followed the teachings of Maharishi Mahesh Yogi in the Transcendental Meditation (TM) movement. They traveled to Italy with Maharishi where they learned the sacred technique of teaching TM. I was taught the meditation technique at a young age and carried it close within me as I grew up. However, the true depth and understanding of spirituality and expansion of consciousness didn't start to fully awaken until November of 2002, when I was seventeen years old, and met the Satguru, Amma (Mata Amritanandamayi). Growing up in this environment created an unwavering faith in the universe. The kind of faith that held me tight with the promise that no matter how slippery and unsteady the world felt with anxiety, everything was going to be OK. There was always the omnipresent support of nature.

Everything in my life was safe, secure, and surrounded by love; nevertheless, as far back as I can remember, I felt debilitating anxiety. My childhood was spent being nervous, fearful, and afraid. I watched my siblings and friends walk into school every day with smiles on their faces, feeling comfortable and safe. I watched them go over to friends' houses for playdates, sleepovers, and birthday parties with excitement. I watched them take art classes, music lessons, play sports, go to summer camps, blissfully enjoying the freedom and fun of childhood. I felt safest watching from the sidelines.

Back in the late 1980s, early 1990s, anxiety was still taboo. You didn't walk into a doctor's office and have them tell you that your child was suffering from a generalized anxiety and panic disorder. It was still believed that in order to have anxiety, something terrible and traumatic had to have happened to you. I had no word to properly describe the insidious disorder I would spend my whole life battling and trying to conquer. I was not introduced to the term "anxiety" until I was fifteen years old—not by a doctor, but by a police officer.

Looking back, sometimes my anxiety was generalized; not linked to anything, anyone, or any specific event. The best way to describe it would be when someone jumps out from around a corner and yells, "Boo!" Your heart starts to race and your stomach jumps into your throat for a split second before your brain makes the connection that there is no real threat and your body starts to calm down and relax. With generalized anxiety, that "Boo!" feeling is constantly there; your adrenaline pumping, the fight or flight mechanism in your brain always turned "on." As a young child without the understanding that this feeling was anxiety, I timidly walked through life full of caution.

At other times, my anxiety would be directly related to something specific. When I was young, nighttime was a big trigger for my anxiety. The anticipation of bedtime was always an ominous cloud that hung over my head. The more the sun set, the more my anxiety awoke. Every night my mother had the arduous task of putting me to bed. She would tuck me under my covers, turn off the lights, turn on the nightlight, and sit on the corner of my bed softly rubbing my back for a few minutes to help me relax into sleep. As she left my room, the door would have to remain wide open. I would lie there with my eyes squeezed tightly closed, pulling the covers over my head and curling myself into the tiniest ball I could possibly create. Like clockwork, the feeling would slowly start to creep into my chest. My heart would start to race, pounding out against my folded knees curled to my chest; feeling and hearing my heart rapidly beating in my ears. My hands, arms, legs, and feet would go tingly and numb. My breathing became shallow and short. It would be at that moment I would jump out of bed, run down the stairs, find my mom and snuggle up next to her. My mother, halfway expecting and waiting for my nightly appearance, would gently take my hand and walk me back to bed as many times as it took for me to stay there and fall asleep.

In addition to having an anxiety disorder, I struggled with panic attacks. Having a panic attack can be one of the scariest feelings your mind and body experience. Someone that has never endured a panic attack before could easily be convinced they were having a heart attack and dying. It can strike out of nowhere and for no particular reason. At other times, there is a direct cause. There have been multiple occasions where I found myself in the emergency room trying to convince the doctors and nurses that something medically serious was happening to me; as if they were overlooking or not finding the real issue. Every single time it was proven to have been a panic attack.

The experience I've had with panic attacks is that it starts and escalates faster than you can blink. There is a feeling of disconnection from my body. My heart races and pounds so fast and hard, I feel as if it could explode. There is a gripping, tightening in my chest that can be suffocating. I can very easily start to hyperventilate. My surroundings can morph and contort causing a spinning dizziness. Sounds can become distant or the opposite, becoming too loud and intense to handle. My hands and feet can tingle and go numb while stiffening and tightening so much so I'm unable to move them. All of these happen simultaneously. Talk about feeling out of control of myself!

Today, new technologies allow doctors to administer brain scans sophisticated enough to read and analyze which parts of the brain over or under function during episodes of anxiety. The disorder is understood much better. Alongside the advancement of medications, proper diet and exercise, tapping into spiritual awareness and practice, and knowledge of self-healing, tools to manage anxiety have become more readily accessible.

The human brain loves patterns, routines, and predictability. The more you train your brain to react a certain way, the more it will default back to that reaction; whether it be anxiety or pure bliss. The brain doesn't discriminate which feeling it will send out to the rest of your body because it looks for the created patterns. It was impossible for me to recognize at the time because I was undiagnosed and untreated, but every time I reacted in a state of anxiety or panic, I was wiring my brain to default back to an anxious, reactive state. Many of my current, existing anxieties were small events that my brain clung to and over time created a snowball effect; growing both the anxiety and pattern of reactive anxiety every time I was exposed to similar situations. It wasn't until I was in my thirties and met my current therapist, that I learned techniques of rewiring and retraining my brain out of a constant, anxious state.

THE BEGINNING

Attending school was one of the hardest daily tasks to accomplish. One of my earliest anxiety memories was when I was four years old and my mother dropped me off at the church nursery school. We pulled up to the church in my mom's old 1980s dark blue Volvo wagon. I was quietly crying in my car seat. "Please, Mommy. I don't want to go! Don't leave me here!" I felt as though the whole world was about to crash down around me. The fear inside my little body felt like a monster clawing its way out of my chest. I knew that once we entered the church doors and walked upstairs, my mother was going to hand me over to the nursery teacher and she'd be gone. My mom walked over to my side of the car, opened the door, and while unbuckling my seat belt said softly, "I always come back for you. You're going to be OK." For a brief few seconds, I felt a sense of calm, relief.

As we walked up the long, paved walkway leading to the main entrance of the church, a tidal wave of panic washed over my body. I must have squeezed my mom's hand a bit tighter because she leaned down and picked me up to carry me the rest of the way inside. We made our way up the red-carpeted stairway, past the big stained-glass cathedral windows. I looked outside, over my mom's shoulder. I could see our car parked at the curb and wanted nothing more than to be back in my car seat, and safe with my mom. But we kept walking up the stairs, down the long echoing hall, and into my classroom. With tears streaming down my face, my mom placed me down, and I immediately hid behind her legs.

The teacher, (who in hindsight was a sweet and patient old lady, but at the time was the devil taking me away from my mother) came walking over to greet me. She kneeled down to my level and said, "Good morning, Whitney. It looks like you need some extra love today." Looking up at my mom, she added, "You can go. I can handle this." And with a loving smile, gently removed my white-knuckled grip from my mom's jeans, turned me toward her, and hugged me tight while my mom left the room. "Now, doesn't that feel better? Now you're ready to play with your friends!" As soon as her grip loosened, I ran over to the third story window to watch my mom strolling down the walkway, get into her car, and drive away. The universe was swallowing me whole.

PROTEST AND TESTING

During my fourth-grade year, I protested going to school. An absolute refusal every morning. Day in and day out, my parents tried to get me to vocalize why going to school was so difficult. I wasn't sure how to describe the way I was feeling inside, so I would get overwhelmed and shut down. I would shrug my shoulders and say, "I don't know," to all their questions. At times I would not speak at all. After so long trying in vain to get me to school and explain why I was so adamant about not attending, they decided to look for professional help.

My general practitioner referred me to a specialized clinic that tested for learning disabilities. The office where the test was administered consisted of a single long white desk in the middle of a room with two chairs on either side. A tall, spindly man took a seat across from me. "There are no right or wrong answers during this test. There is no need to be nervous, OK?" he smilingly said, peering over his round, rimmed glasses that sat on the tip of his large, triangular nose.

I nodded my head to acknowledge I'd heard him and watched as he sorted through a stack of laminated papers. I didn't feel nervous or anxious. Anticipation always got the best of my anxiety; however, in the actual moment, I always performed my best.

The man fished out one of the laminated papers from the stack he held. Printed on it was a forward-facing number four, and next to it was a backward number four. He placed the paper in front of me with an erasable marker. "Can you see a difference between these numbers?" he asked, as he popped the cap off the marker and handed it to me. I grabbed the marker from his spidery fingers and circled the forward-facing number four.

"Very good," he said, as he held up another picture and told me to memorize the objects on the page. He placed the picture face down on the desk, picked up another one, and asked which object(s) were now missing or added to the page.

He had me read short paragraphs out loud and in my head, then explain to him what it was I had just read. He would say a sentence or two and have me repeat it word-for-word back to him. The test continued this way for some time, and at the conclusion, he sat with my parents to discuss the results.

He believed I had a slight auditory processing disorder; meaning it was difficult for me to retain information when being spoken to. I retain information best visually and doing it hands-on. He thought this may be adding to my protest against going to school; however, he didn't think it was the root cause. His job was to test me for cognitive, developmental, and learning disabilities, and he did just that; therefore, not mentioning anything about an anxiety disorder. In the end, he recommended my parents take me to a child psychiatrist so they could determine if my protest was due to emotional distress manifesting as behavioral rebellion.

I was a good child. At that stage of my childhood, there was nothing rebellious about me. I was too anxious to act out in any way.

In young children, logic is not developed in the brain yet so they function from an instinctual, gut-feeling level. To me, school felt scary and unsafe so I didn't want to go. It was that simple to me, and I couldn't understand why my parents didn't get that; much like my parents didn't understand why it was so difficult for me to get up in the morning with my siblings and go to school every day. It was a frustrating battle on both ends.

A few days later, I found myself in a child psychiatrist's office with both my parents. Straightaway, I felt uncomfortable, nervous, judged, talked about, and looked down upon. As my parents shook hands with the pompous-looking man, I sheepishly took a seat on the couch, peering around the room. The office was not 'kid-friendly' but rather a bit intimidating. Bookshelves lined the walls, filled with psychology and self-help books. The white walls held his framed credentials. His desk was neatly arranged in a minimal fashion with a flat desk-calendar covered in sticky notes, highlighted appointments, and a single photo of his family. His wife and children looked like perfectly manicured robots posed for their family portrait; with their polo shirts, and cardigans over their shoulders, their khaki pants, penny loafers, and plastic smiles. I didn't like this guy.

As soon as my parents sat to join me on the couch, I snuggled up close to my mom hiding my face in her lap, curling myself into a tiny "safety-ball". As though, "If I can't see them, then they can't see me."

In a mocking tone the therapist snarked, "Well, I guess Whitney won't be joining us today." Followed by a fake, guttural laugh prompting my parents to join in.

I gritted my teeth, clenched my jaw, and squeezed my body tighter. "What an ass hat!" I thought to myself, still curled up next to my mom.

Anxiety started to take over. A wave of adrenaline rushed through my little body. I wanted nothing more than to get up and run out of the room away from my own self, leaving the anxiety behind, trapped in that room. I listened to what my mother was saying, trying to shift my focus away from the relentless anxiety pumping through my veins.

She started the conversation by explaining all that led us to be in his office, emphasizing the protest of not going to school. She explained everything from how she felt there was something beyond me just being shy, to how I had been virtually attached to her hip since day one.

The psychiatrist asked questions like, "Does Whitney go to friends' houses to play? Does she engage in any extracurricular activities? Is she able to go outside and play on her own? How is her overall attitude toward life? Does she get along with her siblings?" My parents' summary to all the doctor's questions was that I was a happy child, but a scared child. I wanted to join in with what my friends and siblings were engaging in, but something was always holding me back.

The psychiatrist paused, and I could feel his attention shift toward me. He tried speaking to me again but to no avail. Still hiding my face in my mother's lap, curled in my safety- ball, I could hear my father defeatedly say, "This is what happens at home when we try speaking with Whitney about something she doesn't like. There is no communication." My dad was waving his white flag. He didn't know how to help me and was surrendering to the doctor for help.

Along came another drawn-out, dramatic pause from the psychiatrist. I could hear him tapping his pen against his notepad placed on his crossed-legged lap. After letting out a long, unnecessarily loud exhalation, he broke the silence.

He told my parents I was simply choosing to be defiant and testing my boundaries with authority. He said my parents were being too "soft" with me. He told them they had to take control and break the cycle I had created of thinking I was in charge. He told my father to physically remove me from my bed in the morning, if need be, to get me out the door and to school with my sister and brother. He promised them that once I got into an everyday routine and understood the boundaries of authority, I would start attending school without a fight.

I was silently screaming on the inside that the doctor had it all wrong. I wanted to yell at him and my parents that I was scared and afraid all the time and I didn't know why; that I wanted to be *normal* and feel like all of my friends and siblings. I didn't want to be afraid. I wanted someone to help me. I was not *choosing* to be this way. But nothing came out of my mouth.

BACK TO SCHOOL

The next morning, I could hear my mother going from room to room, waking up my brother, then my sister, then making her way toward my room. As she opened my door, I curled under my covers and lay as still as possible. I could feel my mom sit on the edge of my bed and place her hand on my back. She gently reminded me that today was the day I was going back to school. She then got up and left me to get myself out of bed, saying she'd be back in a few minutes to check on me.

I stayed perfectly still under my covers. I wasn't giving in that easily. After my mom's second failed attempt to get me out of bed, she gave me one last chance with the warning that if I wasn't out of bed in five minutes, my father was coming upstairs to get me.

Neither of my parents was ever one for discipline, especially my father. He hadn't experienced an ideal childhood, so when he had children of his own, he promised himself that he would do differently by us. In an extreme sense, he stuck by his word. There was never punishment or consequence for disobedience; therefore, my mother's threat of sending my father upstairs to get me out of bed held no weight.

I stood my ground, hiding under my covers.

I could feel my dad's presence as he walked into my room. The tone in his voice when he demanded I "Get out of bed, NOW," sent a sudden surge of panic through my body. My heart started to race, my chest squeezed the breath out of me, my skin crawled from the inside out. My safety-ball started to feel vulnerable and cracked. My mind shifted from fight to flight. I wanted to jump out of my bed, run from my room away from my parents and find a new hiding place; but my body didn't move. I lay frozen in my bed, gripping my folded knees tighter to my chest.

My dad's final warning to get out of bed came with a countdown from "Three." When he got to "One" I had no idea what to expect. My parents never counted down as a warning for anything. What I thought was the feeling of my father sitting down on my bed next to me was actually him leaning on and gripping my mattress with both his hands. One swift heave and he flipped the mattress on its side, off of the frame, sending me rolling like a bowling ball across my floor.

It took a moment for my brain and body to realize I was now on the floor. My father had never done anything like that before nor did I ever think he would. I unraveled from my safety-ball stretching out flat on my back looking up at my parents, dazed and confused.

The words, "I'm so sorry, I'm so sorry. I'm so sorry" were stuck on repeat playing from my dad's mouth as I pulled myself up off the floor. I stormed out of my room leaving him with the words, "I hate you!"

For the first time in my life, I felt afraid of my own dad. He could feel it and felt horrible. He left me to calm down in the bathroom where I found myself hiding, sitting on the floor, my legs bent to my chest. A few minutes later, I could hear my dad's car leaving our driveway, going to work. I breathed a sigh of relief as I stood up looking at my tear-stained face in the mirror. I splashed my red eyes with cold water before taking a deep breath, unlocking the bathroom door and returning to my bedroom. It was safe to say that day was not the day I would return to school.

My parents weren't sure how to handle this situation. It became obvious that the more they pushed me, the more I pushed back. I have always had a strong personality. I was never one to be told what to do, how to do it, when to do it, why to do it, or where to do it. People called it stubbornness and defiance, but for me, it was a sense of control over my life that otherwise felt as if it was spiraling out of control from anxiety and fear. The less my parents pushed, the more open I became to going back to school. Eventually, in my own time, I made the decision to return to fourth grade and finish the school year. Going back to my classroom felt surprisingly empowering. I had made that decision on my own, for myself.

On the last day of fourth grade, our teacher let the students walk around freely signing each other's year-books. One of the boys wrote in mine, "Whitney, I'm so glad you didn't die of rabies and came back to school."

I turned to one of my girlfriends showing her the queer message, thinking we'd both get a good laugh about it but to my surprise, she responded, "Oh, yeah, someone told the class you had to miss school because you caught rabies from a dog and were in the hospital." Flushed with embarrassment I slapped my yearbook closed and sunk into my desk chair, counting the seconds for the last day of fourth grade to be over.

HIGH SCHOOL (PART 1)

My transition into high school was disastrous, to say the least. The student body count was an overwhelming 3,000. Some classes were packed with over forty kids per one teacher. Walking through the sea of students in the hallways was like pushing your way through a New York City subway station during rush hour.

Skipping class became an everyday occurrence when I'd find myself frozen with anxiety in the empty hallways once everyone else had made their way into their classes. I could not physically force my body to move toward the classroom.

However, I always enjoyed learning. I had always been inquisitive by nature. I loved absorbing as much knowledge and information as possible. In fact, when I reached high school, I was enrolled in honors and advanced placement (AP) classes. It became increasingly frustrating for me to have such a yearning and passion for learning but be too anxious to sit through a single class without panicking.

I was in AP English with one of my good friends who kept me updated on what was being taught. At the time, the class was studying Shakespeare and reading Hamlet.

One day while heading toward the girls locker room to hide from class and catch up on my reading, I bumped into my best friend, Casandra. She was one of those people who did everything super-fast. It was as if she were functioning on fast forward. She walked fast, talked a mile a minute, and couldn't sit still for more than a few seconds.

"Oh! Hey Whit! Where are you going? Why aren't you in class? I'm late to meet my class in the library. In which direction are you walking? We can walk together. You're holding a book. What are you reading? Is it for English?"

She was speaking so quickly I didn't know how she was walking, talking, and breathing simultaneously. When she stopped talking for half a second to focus on the combination of her locker, I inserted quietly, "I'm not going to my class. I'm not feeling up to it." Without skipping a beat, she slammed her locker shut, spun around, grabbed my hand, and led me down the hallway. "Come on. Come with me if you're not going to your class. My class is in the library. The teacher won't even notice you're there, and if he does, he'll just think you're part of the class."

As we found our seats in the library, I slumped down into my chair, opened my book, and held it up in front of my face, hoping not to be spotted as the odd one out by the teacher. To my great relief, he went on teaching the lesson without taking any notice that I wasn't an actual student in his class. I looked around and thought, "The library. Why hadn't I thought to come here before now? Instead, I had been hiding away in the stinky girls locker room or bathrooms. The library is much more suited for me to spend my time."

Casandra and I had met in sixth grade, and despite being opposites in every way imaginable, we were inseparable. She was tall and supermodel-thin. I stood at five feet tall and had curves. She always styled her platinum blonde hair in some fashion. My long, auburn hair was more often than not left unbrushed and messy. She loved makeup, nail polish, pushup bras, and sexy clothes. I didn't care for all the girly things she lusted over. I'd throw on a T-shirt, jeans, and sneakers, and be ready to go. She was loud, outgoing, and loved flirting with boys. I was quiet, shy, and a little awkward. I couldn't even look at boys without blushing. She was an only child and lived with her strict British father in a small, rundown apartment. She only saw her estranged mother once in a while. My home life depicted the "American dream." My parents were happily married with three kids. My dad's salary provided us with a beautiful house, in a nice suburban neighborhood, and supported a cushioned lifestyle. Casandra always had perfect attendance at school and strived to maintain an A-grade average; mainly to appease her rigid father. I'd always admired her academic achievements, especially because I held a high love of learning. But, my (then) undiagnosed anxiety disorders prohibited my ability to make it through a single class.

The more time passed, the braver I got about leaving the school campus during the day. I was too anxious to attend class, so why was I staying in school? When I left campus,

I would walk a few blocks away to the small, brick, public library. I'd make my way to the second floor, and find a seat at the research tables, where I would select a book at random and read. My logic was that I was supposed to be in school learning things I didn't know, so if I picked a random book off the shelf to read, I would be building and expanding my knowledge. Even if it wasn't what was being taught in class. I would sit and read for hours, getting lost in the substance, the facts. I grew a deep love for studying, for education. I wanted to absorb everything there was to know about everything.

The joy of complete freedom during the school day quickly jolted to a stop when teachers started reporting me as 'absent' every day. Soon my parents started being called in for parent-teacher meetings with the principal.

There was one final meeting that pushed both myself and the principal to our breaking points. I was frustrated and angry that no one understood or recognized my crippling anxiety of being in school, and was being labeled as a defiant, disobedient, good-for-nothing teenager.

A part of my anxiety disorder prevented me from vocalizing how I was feeling inside. My brain would shut down, creating a hazy, foggy, spaced-out feeling to the point of not being able to put a proper sentence together. I wanted nothing more than to stand up for myself and let both the principal and my father know that each day I hid in the public library, reading, studying, and teaching myself. I wasn't skipping school to be rebellious and 'stick it to the man', but nothing ever came out of my mouth. I was trapped living my life day in and day out afraid, fearful, overwhelmed, and no one, not even doctors were helping me. I felt left to fend for myself. I felt alone and lost. Eventually, all the fear and anxiety started to manifest into resentment and anger.

On this particular day, I walked into the principal's office where my father was awaiting my arrival with a zero-fucks-given attitude. The principal sat across from my father and me at his desk, wearing a black, clownishly oversized suit. His arms were crossed on top of his pot belly big enough to keep him from pulling his chair in toward the table.

I sank down into the chair next to my dad, crossed my arms in the same manner as the principal and glared into his eyes across from me. Not the best way to enter into a meeting about my own delinquency, but I was an upset fourteen-year-old child who felt unheard and disappointed in the world. The principal cleared his throat and led the meeting with, "Well, we all know why we're here this morning." Followed by an authoritative boom of, "Explain yourself!"

My dad looked over at me and nodded as if to give me the green light to speak up for myself. Now was my chance. There was so much I wanted to say, explain, and defend myself; however, what came out of my mouth was quite the opposite of what I should have calmly stated. I frustratedly shouted, "I don't see the point in school. The teachers teach me nothing. I educate myself better than any teacher in this entire school. I have more knowledge than they do. You don't know anything about me yet you call me into your office and speak to me as if you know everything. You're an asshole of a principal!" My father cut my rant short by placing his hand on my leg, looking over at me and gently saying, "Enough." Even though my father never fully understood me, he always had my back. Looking back at him, I shut my mouth and took a few deep breaths to re-center myself.

The principal, on the other hand, was doing anything but calming down. Wide-eyed, he stared back at me in disbelief. His face turned redder by the second as if steam were about to start pouring from his ears. His gaze shifted from me to my father and snapped, "Do you see what we're dealing with here? Your daughter is a disgrace. The arrogance and blatant disrespect on this one. She will never amount to anything! Thinking she is bigger, better, and smarter than everyone in this school and she's FAILING the ninth grade! She can't even make it to a single class throughout the day." Now cutting the principal off in the middle of his rant, my father stood up and said, "Enough! This is the example you're modeling for the children of this school?"

I stood up next to my dad and staring directly at the principal remarked, "See, Dad? He's an asshole."

Without words, my dad simply pointed at the door, and I more than gladly left the office. A few moments later, my dad met me in the hallway and together we walked holding hands out of the school and toward his car.

My father wasn't impressed by my attitude or the way I'd handled the meeting but was in total agreement that the principal was unquestionably an ass. Before driving home, my dad made me look him into his eyes as he told me, "You are NOT a disgrace. You are NOT stupid. And you CAN be anything you put your mind to. You also can't skip school every day just because you think school is stupid."

I smiled at my dad for halfway understanding my situation. He leaned over, kissed my forehead and drove both of us home. When we pulled into our driveway my dad turned to me and slyly remarked, "Hey, I bet you are smarter than the teachers in that school. The best revenge is to show them that you are." Breathing a sigh of relief, I smiled and went inside.

Because of truancy, I ended up failing my ninth-grade year. My parents knew my intellect and saw my potential; however, they also recognized my struggle attending school from a very young age and wanted to help me succeed academically any way they could.

HIGH SCHOOL (PART 2)

Toward the tail end of my freshman year, already aware of my need to repeat the ninth grade, my parents looked into alternative schools that could accommodate my needs academically and socially. After looking at a few private schools, I ended up falling in love with one particular prep school. This school was noted for its academic excellence. There was a lengthy interview process for getting accepted into the school. Face to face interviews with the headmaster and school board, alongside written tests.

Waiting outside for our arrival on the first interview day was the headmaster of the prep school. I quickly recognized he was a Sikh, as he was dressed in all-white linen garments, with a white turban upon his head. His eyes sparkled with a sweet softness when he smiled through his salt-and-pepper wizardly beard. Any anxiety of anticipation for the interview disappeared when I was greeted by him. He was warm and inviting. He emanated a sense of reassuring calm.

I walked into the office confident in my interview skills and proving my intelligence to the school board. After the first of three sit-down interviews, I was asked to write an essay, explaining why I should be chosen over all the other applicants. I was walked into a quiet, small office where I had one hour to compose my convincing essay.

It was as if the divine intervened at that exact moment and allowed my lifetime's worth of pent-up, vocally unexplainable anxiety flow openly onto the pages. What I was feeling all those years on the inside, was effortlessly written into words. I wrote how difficult it was for me to go to school every day ever since I could remember. I wrote how I felt afraid, nervous as if I was crawling out of my own skin every second of every day; and how that made me feel alone and scared. I wrote how I would skip class and hide, studying in the library every day but I never told anyone where I would go. Partly because I didn't think anyone would believe me, partly because I loved reading, and research, taking notes, and absorbing as many facts and information as possible, and partly because I didn't want to be found. I explained how I would benefit greatly from going to the school because of the smaller student to teacher ratio. How the academics were advanced and would challenge me in the ways I needed and wanted. I finished my essay, stating how I had been labeled the "problem child" but I wasn't, and it wasn't a pleasant reputation to have, nor one I wanted to uphold.

The headmaster came to retrieve the essay as my writing hour came to a close. He led my parents and me outside where he invited us to explore the campus while he and the school board reviewed my essay. As I wandered around the campus, I thought about how empowering it felt to write down all the bottled-up emotions that had been stuck inside of me for so long. I had never used writing as a form of self-therapy and that magical day released from me a lifetime of frustration, sadness, fear, and anxiety, onto paper. For the first time in forever, I felt free.

I strolled past the glistening lake surrounded by trees in the center of the campus, imagining myself as a student walking to class. I looked inside the classrooms of the towering brick buildings sectioned off by wings for each academic subject. Nestled in the woods were two small cottage-style buildings; one, the library and the other, art and photography. Looping back around the lake were boys and girls dormitories. Students from all over the world were enrolled in this school.

Standing in front of the dorms, I took a long, slow, deep breath in. As I let out my exaggerated exhalation, I saw the headmaster walking toward me. Collecting my parents and me, we walked together back to his office.

The headmaster took his seat, and with a warm smile said, "We have discussed your interview and are all in agreement to expedite your acceptance into our school. We formally extend an in-person invitation to join us here this fall" (no second and third oral interview required). With a huge sigh of relief and gratitude, I shook the principal and school board members' hands, thanking them, and left the office.

While driving away from the campus my dad peered back at me through the rearview mirror saying, "I knew you would get in, Whit. Now prove those assholes from public school wrong, eh?"

SUMMER VACATION GONE TERRIBLY WRONG (PART 1)

The summer started off on a high note. Having been accepted into the prep school was my shot at redemption. It wasn't a bother that I would repeat the ninth grade. It was a fresh, new start. However, as summer wore on, things quickly took a sharp right turn.

Casandra started showing interest in experimenting with drugs and alcohol and doing more than just flirting with boys. All of these things intimidated me, and up to that point in time, I had shied away from experiencing any of them.

One day while over her house, and her dad at work, she invited Drew, an older boy she liked, to hang out with us. As we awaited his arrival, my anxiety quickly took over. My heart started to race, the room spun around me, and the all too familiar rush of adrenaline exploded through my veins. The suffocating grip, tightening and crawling its way out of my thumping chest made me want to run away from myself.

I ran into Casandra's bathroom and locked the door behind me. As I stood at the sink, splashing cold water on my face, and telling my reflection in the mirror, "I'm OK," I heard her doorbell ring. "Shit!" I whispered out loud to myself. "I should just go home. What excuse do I use to get out of here? I'll tell her I'm not feeling well and leave." I took a deep breath, unlocked the bathroom door, and quietly made my way to the living room where I found her and said boy making out on her couch.

"Oh Lord, ew! No, thanks!" I thought to myself, as I grabbed my coat and headed for the door. Before I could make my escape, Drew called out, "Yo! Where are you going, shy one?"

My friend's head popped up from under him to see what was happening. Spinning around thinking, "Damn it! Quick Whitney, think fast." I muttered back, "Um, I'm just not feeling so well. I'm going to walk home." My heart was racing, hands shaking, and I was ready to dart toward the door.

He quickly replied, "Wait!" as he jiggled around in his pocket pulling out a long, white, hand-rolled, crinkled up joint. "This will fix you right up. It'll make you feel better on all levels, my friend."

I had never seen a joint in real life before let alone lit and smoked one.

"Oh yay! Come on, Whit! Come sit with us. He's right, it'll make you feel so much better. I promise!" Casandra patted the couch cushion next to her inviting me over. I felt as if there were no way out now.

"Here," Drew smilingly passed me the joint. "The guest of honor can have the first hit."

Drew was tall, dark, and handsome, and he knew it. He ran his fingers through the waves of his thick, brown hair, and bit down on his bottom lip. "Don't be scared, it's all good," he persuaded me with a wink from his deep brown eyes.

I could feel my face flush bright red. "Shit, shit, shit!" I thought to myself frozen on the couch, joint and lighter in hand.

A few moments later, Casandra snatched the joint from me, stuck it in her mouth, turned to her boy crush and stated, "Whit's a noobie at smoking weed. We have to teach her." She lit the joint and exhaled a cloud of pot smoke with a giant cough. I thought my stomach was going to jump into my throat and my heartbeat out of my chest. I supposed this was what peer pressure felt like. With shaky hands, I took the joint from her and took a tiny puff. As I exhaled the smoke, I thought, "OK, this isn't so bad. So far so good."

The more the joint was passed around between us, the more relaxed I became. The unrelenting cloud of fear and anxiety that had plagued me everywhere I went suddenly started to dissipate. The endless stream of "what if's" in my head began to quiet. I sat soundlessly and still feeling the tranquility inside my body, thinking, "Wow, is this what 'normal' feels like?" I could hear Casandra and Drew giggling, goofing off, and crunching on endless munchies, but I was so absorbed in this brand-new feeling of calm, all I wanted to do was be still and feel the moment. I closed my eyes and tried my hardest to safe-lock the feeling in my brain forever.

Summer rolled on and we started hanging around Drew more often. The more we saw of him, the more of his friends we were introduced to. These kids weren't from the town we lived in. They came from poor neighborhoods and broken homes. They were always in survival mode; some homeless runaways. They stank of sweat, cigarettes, and alcohol. Their clothes were ripped and filthy, with patterns of pot leaves and anarchy symbols; their hair in dreadlocks and mohawks. They were the complete opposite of anything I'd ever seen or hung around. I always felt a little unsettled around them, but I hung out with them because they had the connection to weed; and, smoking weed calmed my anxious brain. I was self-medicating the only way I had successfully figured out up to that point.

The group of us would take the train into Boston and roam around, down Boylston Street and Mass Ave. We would drift in and out of the stores on Newbury Street, and putts around Harvard Square. I'd follow them around, waiting for one of them to score a bag of weed and find somewhere to sit and roll a joint.

I'd sit around, watching them all drink themselves into a stupor. I was always too afraid and turned off from getting drunk. I saw how it changed people and made them feel, and I never wanted to participate. More often than not, I wanted to walk away from them, jump on the next train home and disappear; but then I wouldn't have any connection to the one thing that made me feel normal, and I didn't want to let that go. Although my gut was telling me these kids were bad news and it would end in disaster, I pushed the feeling down and away.

My parents planned a weekend getaway in Canada after they dropped my brother, Luke off at sleep-away summer camp. They left my sister Heather and me home alone. As most teenagers would, Heather planned a house party with her best friend, Sara, the night after my parents left. Heather's friends flooded into the house, carrying beer and alcohol as if entering a frat party. They scattered themselves around the house and backyard. People were beginning to get drunk, loud, and obnoxious. The more time passed, the more overwhelmed and irritated I became. I hid in my room and called Casandra over to keep me company.

Remembering how freeing and grounding it was writing that essay at the school interview, I put my earbuds in, pressed play on my iPod, picked up my journal, and started to write.

Just as I was getting into the groove of writing and feeling a sense of calm, there came a knock on my bedroom door. For a brief moment, I regretted calling Casandra over but it was too late to change my mind; she was already there. I rolled off my bed and moseyed over to my door to let her in. To my surprise, she'd brought Drew with her, and three of the motley kids she and I had been hanging out with that summer. Irritated that I hadn't been asked if she could bring these types of kids to my house, I reluctantly invited them all into my room.

We sat down cross-legged in a circle on the floor, ready to light a joint, when two of my sister's friends barged into my room. They were stumbling drunk, and one of them was flapping a brown paper lunch bag around, telling us there was weed inside, and asking if we wanted to buy it from them. I took the bag from the drunkard, opened it and didn't need to look inside before smelling that it was dried oregano. Crumpling up the bag and throwing it back at him, I snapped, "Get your drunk asses out of my room!"

Before giving him and his friend a chance to leave, I pushed passed them and ran downstairs to find Heather. I was expecting my sister to tell her friends to lay off me, but she did the exact opposite and defended them, saying they were just having a little fun. No harm, no foul. Super frustrated and disappointed in her, I ran upstairs to find her friends still in my room. The two piss-drunk guys were bribing one of my friends, Mark, with money to beat up another guy at the party who had stolen one of their girlfriends.

Mark was one of the homeless runaways in the group. He was ruggedly handsome without ever trying. All the girls had a crush on Mark. He was tall and thin, but muscular. He had shaggy, dirty blonde hair, and eyes as blue as the sky. He was rough and tough and seemed to be the leader in the group of friends. His clothes were always dirty and ripped, and he always stank of beer and cigarettes.

Thinking the bribe was a complete absurdity, and assuming Mark would feel the same, it was to my complete and utter surprise, and disgust that he grabbed the money out of the guy's hand saying, "Yeah, alright, I'll do it. Where is this guy?" Before I had time to think my body was rushing in-between my sister's friends and Mark.

"What the actual fuck, you guys? You cannot send him to do your dirty work! And what the hell is wrong with you, taking money to beat someone up who literally has nothing to do with you?"

Mark put his hands on my shoulders and while physically moving me out of his way replied, "When you don't know when the next time is you're going to eat, you do what you have to for some cash."

Everyone but me and one of the girls, Ashley, disappeared from my room, with my sister's friends leading the way. Ashley was a runaway, too. She and I got along well. She dressed in handmade, hippy-looking clothes and had long, stick-straight brown hair down to her hips. She was like me in the way of not having much interest in girly things. She was a wild, free spirit, with a big heart.

Ashley asked if I was OK, but her voice was in the distance, as I paced back and forth, my hands on either side of my head.

"Shit! Shit! Shit!" I yelled out loud as panic set in. "How do I fix this? I can't fix this. This is so fucked!" My heart felt like it was going to explode pounding so fast and hard out of my chest. The adrenaline pumping through my body sent me into flight mode. I grabbed my sweatshirt and the joint off my bed.

In a worried tone, Ashley asked, "Where are you going?"

Ignoring Ashley's concern, I ran downstairs toward the front door, ducking and dodging my way through the gang of my sister's friends breaking up the fight.

"Oy! Where do you think you're going? Whitney!" Heather yelled over the chaos.

I didn't flinch. I just kept running. As I ran down my street, I found my dog Brandy, a giant Bernese Mountain dog, lying on a neighbor's lawn looking panicked and scared. She had escaped the madness of the house and run, too. I was so glad to see her, I dropped on the ground next to her, wrapped my arms around her neck and began to weep. "It's OK, Brandy. It's OK," I told her over and over as I cried and squeezed her tighter. Taking a few deep breaths, I unraveled my iron grip from around my dog and with a few sweet kisses from her, I sat up, wiped the tears from my face and lit my joint. Sitting alone in the dark, talking out loud to Brandy, I resolved that I wasn't going to speak to my 'friends' anymore. They were nothing but terrible trouble.

Not a moment after I came to that conclusion, I could hear the group of my friends walking down the street toward me. Looking up at the pitch-black star-covered sky, speaking to the universe, I whispered, "Seriously?" They were so engrossed in their conversation about the fight that had just taken place, I hoped they wouldn't notice me and Brandy sitting quietly on the lawn as they walked by.

They were a few steps past us when my dog whimpered and wagged her tail at the passersby. "Damn it, Brandy. You blew our cover!" I whispered as the group spun around tracing the noise behind them.

"Whitney! There you are, little one! We've been kicked out of your house and have set sail to…to…well, wherever the wind takes us!" Mark stammered.

"We're off to Neverland!" Joey obnoxiously chimed in; one of the boys from the group who seemed to always be at Mark's side. He was a small, scrawny-looking teenager, with bright orange hair, freckles and acne all over his rat-like face, and metal braces that filled his whole mouth.

"Shhhhh! God damn it! It's 4 am and we're literally standing on someone else's lawn. Are you trying to get the cops called on you?" I whisper-yelled at all of them.

"Alright, alright, calm down Tinkerbell. Come on, walk with us," Mark replied as he wrapped his arm around my shoulder prompting me to go with them.

Then and there, I should have told the lot of them to fuck off but I was scared to go home, so I took Brandy by the collar and followed the group down the street.

We made our way across the golf course I used as a dog park and shortcut across town, settling at the far end of a manmade lake. Taking a seat on the footbridge that stretched to either side of the water, I dangled my legs through the posts, lying back to stare at and get lost in the night sky.

Mark came over and sat next to me. I cringed inside and wished for him to disappear. Instead, he opened his stupid mouth saying, "So, me and the gang decided to road trip it up to Michigan. All we need is a car. You game?"

My stomach rolled, I clenched my teeth, and sitting up shouted at him, "Am I game? Get the hell out of here with that shit. No, I am NOT 'game.'" I'd had enough. I wasn't like those kids. They were dirty, scummy, runaways with no respect for anyone or anything. Standing up, I grabbed my dog's collar. "Heel, Brandy. We're going home."

"Whoa, whoa, whoa!" Mark said, following after me. "Calm down, little one. You don't need to come with us. We just need your car."

I knew he was talking about my sister's car. They had already done enough damage and the more he spoke the more pissed off I got. "Fuck off!" my voice echoed through the empty golf course.

Everyone else in the group spun around to see what was going on. Casandra and Ashley ran over to me, leaving the boys behind. "I'm done, you guys. I just want to go home and forget that tonight ever happened. Quit following me!" I snapped.

Brandy and I made our way up my street as the sun was rising and all my sister's friends were leaving my house. Standing at the end of the driveway was my sister's boy-friend, Stephen (now my brother-in-law) as if awaiting my arrival. The moment our eyes met, I broke down sobbing uncontrollably.

He grabbed and pulled me in for a tight squeeze saying, "Hey, it's OK. Everyone and everything is OK. We all fuck up. We all still love you."

I let myself sink deep into his hug and for those few seconds, I felt safe.

Everything went right back to shit when I looked up from Stephen's hug and saw Heather a few yards behind him, glaring at me from the front door as if she were mur-dering me with her eyes. I dropped my head, dropped my shoulders, sighed a here-we-freakin-go sigh, and trudged my way up the driveway. I wasn't sure what Heather had told Stephen so the blame of the party and fight was placed on me. Heather and Sara were the ones that planned the house party, the house was swamped with *their* friends, and *their* friends bribed Mark to start a fight. I was too exhausted physically and mentally to defend myself, so I silently walked past my sister, up the stairs, and finally crawled into my bed, where I could sleep and forget about the world for a while.

SUMMER VACATION GONE TERRIBLY WRONG (PART 2)

Over the years, my bed had turned into my safe place. Rolled into a tight ball, covers over my head, I would turn invisible and disappear from the world. Curling up in my bed early that morning after the party was heaven. I slept the day away until I was woken up by little "tinks" from pebbles hitting my window. My stomach turned. I didn't want to come out from hiding under the sheets. The longer I ignored the pebbles, the more of them hit my window. I thought I had made myself clear the night before when I told the group to fuck off. I hadn't thought they'd have the audacity to show up at my house after what happened the night before at the party.

I peeked out my window to see the three runaways from the group, Mark, Joey, and Ashley standing on my driveway. Casandra and Drew must have gone home to crash out and catch up on sleep after I left them on the golf course before the sun rose that morning. These three apparently didn't care because there they were, standing on my driveway. I opened my window and yelled for them to get off my driveway, and to meet me down the street in a few minutes. While quickly throwing on jeans and a T-shirt, I plotted how to get rid of them once and for all.

Walking down the street toward the group of misfits, all I could think about was getting them away from me and my house. "My parents are coming home tonight," I lied, hoping it would scare them off.

"Oh yeah?" Mark asked, "Well, we're leaving for Michigan tonight anyway, little one. We just wanted to come and say bye. And see if maybe you had changed your mind about lending us your car?"

I knew there was an agenda beyond wanting to say goodbye. My entire being filled with rage. "Lend you my car? First of all, it's not lending, it's STEALING. Secondly, it's not my car! And lastly, NO! You cannot STEAL my sister's car! I'm going home. Don't follow me!"

Leaving the three of them in the distance, I could hear Joey's weaselly voice saying to Mark, "Don't worry, we'll convince her tonight." My guts twisted into knots. I knew that wouldn't be the last of them. I walked home as fast as I could, not looking back.

When I got home, I locked myself in my room, grabbed my journal and started to write. Once I started writing, I couldn't stop. I wrote about resenting ever meeting that group of kids. I wrote how awful I felt about recent decisions I'd made involving those friends. I wrote how scared I had been the night before at my sister's party and how alone I'd felt. I wrote how I wasn't going to be friends with them anymore and how I was looking forward to the fall and starting at the new school so I could leave the summer behind me. I wrote until my hand cramped and ached; until I physically couldn't write anymore. I wrote until there were no more words left to write.

The closer to nightfall it became, the greater my anxiety grew. I paced around my house, restless. My mind couldn't stop replaying what Joey had said earlier. "Don't worry. We'll convince her tonight." I knew they were coming back.

The words, "Heather, I'm scared. This group of crazy kids is trying to steal your car and I don't know what to do. I need your help. I need my sister" were on the tip of my tongue but I couldn't force them out.

I had no appetite for supper. I ran a hot bath and lay as still as I could, watching the pounding of my heart create little ripples under the water. I lay there until the water was cold. I pulled myself out of the tub, letting the water drip onto the floor. Goosebumps rose all over my shivering body, and my lips were blue from the cold air drying my wet body. I stared at myself in the mirror. Tears welled in my eyes. "You are strong. You are brave. Everything is going to be OK," I told my reflection a few times before finally grabbing a towel to warm myself.

I yelled down the stairs to Heather that I was going to bed early and locked myself in my room. I had no idea when or if the group of kids was going to show up. I closed the windows and blinds in my room and turned off the light. My plan was to completely ignore them if they showed up, to act as if I wasn't home. I figured if there was no response from me, they'd have no choice but to go away.

Exhausted physically and emotionally from the past few days, I fell straight to sleep. Around 3 am, I woke up to my heart racing, in a pool of my own sweat. Disoriented, I sat up trying to center myself. My entire being froze and tightened up when I realized what had woken me up. Someone was knocking on my bedroom window. They had scaled the trellis on the side of the house and climbed onto the balcony outside my window. These kids were incorrigible! I didn't dare move. I held my breath and squeezed the covers over my head. "Ignore them and they'll go away. They'll have no choice if I don't respond to them," I told myself, lying as still as possible listening for any voices or movement outside.

After what felt like an eternity, the knocking suddenly stopped. I could hear whoever was outside my window leap off the balcony and hit the ground. I breathed a huge sigh of relief thinking they had finally given up.

It was a few minutes later that I heard footsteps coming up the stairs toward my bedroom. They were in the house. They had broken into my house. My body immediately went into a panic. My eyes shot wide open; my heart started to race. I thought I was going to throw up. I was frozen like a deer in headlights under my covers. My doorknob jiggled followed by taps on my door. "Pssst…Whitney…Wake up," the voice from the other side of the door whispered. I could tell it was Mark's voice trying to get my attention. I was afraid if I continued to ignore him, he would go to my sister's room next. So, I forced my frozen-scared body out of bed and opened my door. Mark stood in front of me, holding my sister's car keys. My adrenaline took over and I reacted in fight-mode. Protecting my territory, I felt as big and strong as an angry bear. Before Mark had a chance to say anything I growled, "Did you just fucking break into my house and are now flashing my sister's car keys at me? There is legitimately something wrong with you! Get out of my house, NOW!" I reached up to grab the keys from his hands but he raised them above my head like an annoying child playing keep away.

"The keys were sitting on the kitchen counter, downstairs," Mark said. "I came in through the living room window."

I wasn't sure why he had come upstairs to wake me up and show me that he had the keys. Was he trying to intimidate me? Was he trying to prove that he had won? The fight in me quickly started to shift back to sheer panic and all I wanted was this asshole out of my house. I started to feel as though I was fighting a losing battle. Not only was I intimidated by the size of this guy, but he had just broken into my house and was flaunting in my face he was about to steal my sister's car.

"Do you realize you're incriminating yourself by telling me exactly what you just did? Your dumb ass needs to go! NOW!" I tremblingly whisper-shouted at him, pointing down my stairs. He stared at me for a moment looking almost as if he felt the slightest bit of remorse before turning around toward the stairs.

He replied, "Nice knowing you, little one," and off he went.

I squeezed my eyes tightly closed, my hands held to my chest, and took in a few deep breaths. Tiptoeing down the stairs, I checked to make sure no one was still in the house. When I got to the living room, I walked over to the window that was left wide open; the outside screen ripped off. I reached up to close the window and could hear Heather's car starting at the end of the driveway. I froze and listened until I could no longer hear the car in the distance. They were gone.

Tears flooding down my face, I sank to the floor where I sat for a while replaying what had just happened in my head. I knew both my sister and parents were going to kill me for this and in the same breath, I had felt cornered and bullied into letting it happen. I felt so lost, so alone, and so disappointed in myself. I pulled myself up off the floor and back upstairs into bed. I sank deep under the covers on my bed, curled my knees to my chest, squeezing my arms around them tight, and cried myself to sleep.

The first stroke of dawn's light immediately woke me up. Waves of panic rippled up my spine. I hid in my room until my sister and Sara realized her car was missing from the driveway. They flung my bedroom door open demanding I tell them where Heather's car was. Then and there was the perfect time to tell them what happened the night before, but I was scared. My brain shut down. I couldn't put a sentence together to speak to my sister. The room started spinning around me. My heart beat out of my chest. My hands, which at first were tingling and numb, started to curl into themselves stiffening to where I couldn't uncurl them. I was breathing a mile a minute, beginning to hyperventilate. I felt as though I was going to pass out. My sister and Sara glared at me waiting for my response and all I could mutter was, "I think you should call the police."

Slamming my bedroom door behind them, the pair ran downstairs to call the police and report Heather's car stolen.

I flopped myself off my bed onto my back, on the floor. I spread my limbs out like a starfish and told myself to breathe, over and over, until my breathing started to slow down. Eventually, my heart slowed its rapid thumping and my blood started circulating properly, allowing my hands to uncurl and relax. I started to reconnect with and feel in control of my body again. I lay there, motionless, staring blankly up at the ceiling until I heard the doorbell ring. The police had arrived.

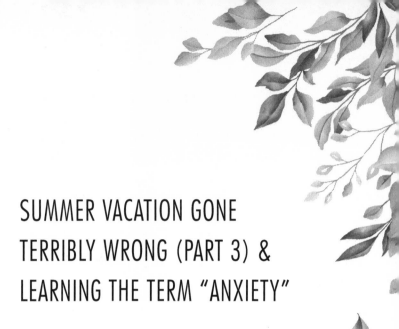

SUMMER VACATION GONE TERRIBLY WRONG (PART 3) & LEARNING THE TERM "ANXIETY"

I treaded lightly down the stairs and sank into the couch next to Heather and Sara. A few officers were outside dusting the break-in window for fingerprints, while a couple of officers were preparing to ask the three of us the details of what happened. There was another chance for me to speak up, and tell everyone my side of the story. Instead, I sat frozen next to my sister not saying a word. Her voice faded into the distance as my focus shifted to an officer telling another that Mark's fingerprints had been found and identified in their system. The officer turned and asked us if we recognized Mark's name. I leaned back into the couch, as a rush of panic took over.

An older, veteran office recognized what was happening with me. His stout, round body bent down in front of me and gently said, "It's going to be OK, honey. Try looking at my face and nothing else. Just focus on me and ignore everything else that is going on. Can you try to do that for me?"

Taken by surprise that someone understood and acknowledged how I was feeling, I listened to and followed what he said.

"Keep your eyes focused on me. No one else is around. Take a slow, deep breath in through your nose and exhale really slowly through your mouth. Keep breathing like this. I'm not going anywhere. Focus on my face and your breath."

I stared into the officer's soft eyes and breathed as instructed.

"You're having a panic attack and we need to calm you down. You're doing just fine. Stay focused on me, honey," the officer reassured me with his thick Boston accent. "Have you ever experienced anxiety like this before?" I nodded my head yes and tremblingly replied, "But I never knew it was anxiety."

Anxiety. That was the first time anyone had ever put a word and meaning to the pestilent shadow that had stalked me my whole life. All the doctors, therapists, and testing now seemingly done in vain over the years was explained in that single moment by a police officer.

"It took me going to war and making it home alive for someone to tell me I was experiencing anxiety. I know how you are feeling and I promise you, you are OK. You are safe. How are you doing now?" The silver-haired policeman asked, still kneeling down in front of me. My arms wrapped around the officer in the tightest thank-you embrace I'd ever given anyone.

"I'll take that as you're feeling better. You're alright, kid." The kind officer winked at me while standing up and returning to his fellow officers.

The second the policemen left my house, I raced upstairs to my room and grabbed the dictionary and thesaurus off my bookshelf. I flipped to the page that held the definition of "anxiety."

Anxiety—Noun: A feeling of worry, nervousness, or unease, typically about an imminent event or something with an uncertain outcome.

I grabbed my thesaurus and found "anxiety." *Synonyms for anxiety—worry, concern, apprehension, unease, fear, nervousness. Antonyms for anxiety—calmness, serenity.*

Psychiatry definition—A nervous disorder characterized by a state of excessive uneasiness and apprehension, typically with compulsive behavior or panic attacks.

I reached back to the dictionary and looked up panic. *Panic—sudden uncontrollable fear or anxiety, often causing wildly unthinking behavior.*

Fueled by a sense of utter relief and sudden understanding, I needed to satisfy the wonderment ignited within me to understand myself. All those years I'd felt misunderstood, misdiagnosed, lost, and alone; but all of that was shifting to empowerment and creating space to grow because now I had the magic word, anxiety. I picked up my journal and started to write. I expressed how I knew the universe had sent me that police officer to finally explain what I had been experiencing for so long. I wrote how thankful I was and how free the knowledge of a single word made me feel. The lock on the cage that held me captive my whole life had just been picked and the door opened for me to step out, stretch my wings, and explore the world through a new pair of eyes.

I decided I needed to arm myself with as much information as possible about anxiety and panic attacks. I darted down the stairs, passed my sister and Sara, toward the front door. "Where do you think you're going?" Heather yelled as I dashed past her. "Mom and Dad are coming home tonight. I need to know where you are!"

Focused on my target, I completely ignored her, ran outside, jumped on my bike, and peddled as fast as I could toward the library.

I ran up the library stairs to the place I felt most comfortable; where I had found refuge the previous school year. I asked the librarian where I could find any and all books about anxiety. As we walked through the different sections, I grabbed books off the shelves until my arms were overflowing. I made my way to a table, splashing the books down, and spreading them out to sift through them.

I sat for hours, reading through and bookmarking pages. I scanned through medical books that explained the wiring of the brain of a person with anxiety and panic disorders; comparing and matching the symptoms and behaviors listed to my own. I took notes from self-help books and memoirs. There was an overwhelming amount of information to read and absorb, so I made photocopies to bring home and dissect in greater detail.

The librarian, unbeknownst to me, had been curiously observing my scrupulous and somewhat frantic research. She walked over to the table where I was sitting and took a seat across from me. She pulled her Rapunzel-long, black hair up and out of the way, so as to not sit on it, and quietly looked at me through her thick, oversized spectacles. Without any inquiry of why I was doing what I was, she warmly smiled at me saying, "You are very brave. You are safe." Then, she stood back up and strolled back to her desk. It was as if the universe had intervened, sending me the police officer and librarian to teach and support me at the moment I needed it the most. I sat quiet and still for a moment, took a deep breath, and thanked God for helping me.

I was afraid to go home after leaving the library. I knew my sister was there worried about where I had run off to, and I didn't want to voluntarily walk into that confrontation. So, I hopped on my bike and peddled toward the Charles River. The docile, babbling path of the river wrapped and wound its way through my town. I jumped off my bike at the wood's edge, pushing it next to me as I made my way down to the bank of the water. I took a seat on a bed of freshly fallen pine needles, and dipped my feet into the cold, gently flowing water. I inhaled the intoxicating scent of the forest.

I was alone. A place I hadn't been in a long time. A place I needed to be. I lay back and stared up through the tree branches, watching the wisps of clouds float by. Seeing the ever-changing sky, feeling the river's water stream over and past my feet, and listening to the coming and going of birdsong. It was nature's reminder that nothing in life is stagnant. There is a constant shift and change. In that moment, change was more than welcome. I closed my eyes to meditate in the calm I had found in the woods. Repeating my mantra (the sacred word you repeat during meditation) over and over again, I slowly dove into the transcending silence absorbing the tranquility while it lasted.

The next day, when my parents got home, my initial reaction was to run up and hug them, never letting go. I wanted nothing more than to show them all the research I had found about anxiety at the library. Instead, the fear of my father's wrath and looming dread of what was to come had me silently hiding in my room. I was lying in my bed, praying to the universe that my parents take mercy on me when I heard my father's knock on the bedroom door. I was convinced that was the end of my existence. My brain flatlined. I was paralyzed from thoughts and words. My dad's tension was tangible; the energy in the room was thick. Every step my dad took toward me, the harder my heart thumped. He sat down on the edge of my bed and without asking if I was OK, without asking my side of the story, without any sense of warmth or compassion stated, "This is some serious shit, Whit. Your 'friends' are being charged with grand theft auto. The officer I spoke to told me you could have been arrested and charged with being an accomplice but they took pity on you. Is that what you want? Do you want to get arrested, thrown in jail and grow up without parents or your brother and sister?"

I found myself (again) screaming on the inside but no words came forth. All I could manage to sputter out was, "No, I don't want any of that." My head hung low, tears clouding my eyes, and I gripped my bedsheets tightly from frustration. My father stood up and headed for the door. Before leaving he turned to look at me. "I hope this is the last of your crazy shit. You've put us through enough. Don't you EVER scare your mother like that again!" And with that, he shut my door and left me feeling more alone than when my parents were out of town.

My dad had riddled me full of guilt. I mentally beat myself black and blue for disappointing my parents, at the same time overflowing with frustration and anger that no one seemed to care enough to ask my side of the story. I was prosecuted and convicted with a guilty verdict with no fair trial by my own family. Above all, I was beginning to resent myself for feeling trapped inside my own head. When the anxiety took control, I was physically unable to vocalize what I wanted so badly to say. I wanted to stick up for myself. I wanted to share my side of the story whether it was welcomed by my parents or not. Alas, the anxiety had once again reigned victoriously. I picked up my journal, which had become a good friend, an ally. All the words that were stuck inside flowed freely onto the blank pages.

PREP SCHOOL (PART 1)

The summer closed on a dramatic note as fall made its entrance. Back-to-school season was crisp in the air. Excitement and nerves bubbled through me as I prepared for the first day at my new school.

On student orientation day, my father drove me to campus. We turned onto the long, cobblestone driveway, lined with towering pine and oak trees that created a tunnel effect leading to the administrative building. When we entered the drop-off queue, he reached into his pants pocket and pulled out a neatly folded piece of paper. With a subtle nod followed by an encouraging wink, he placed the paper in my hand.

"I'll see you after school. You'll have a good first day," he confidently told me.

I slipped the paper in my pocket, grabbed my backpack and jumped out of the car. I apprehensively made my way toward the crowd of new students that anxiously awaited the start of orientation. Once I settled myself among the crowd, I reached into my pocket and retrieved my father's note. "At last, at last, the past is past. I've broken free and won! Now it's time to love myself, and really have some fun!" Smiling to myself, I refolded the note, shoved it back in my pocket, and was ready to take on the day.

I quickly fell in love with everything about the prep school. The small student to teacher ratio allowed the teachers to tailor lesson plans for each student's personal needs. In addition, the small class sizes created a close bond between students; there was a family-like support system. The academics were advanced and challenging, supporting my love of learning. Unfortunately, as the school year rolled on, my anxiety crept back with vengeance. Waking up to go to school every day became increasingly difficult. Contrary to my reaction at public school (running away from campus each day to the library), I forced myself to be present and be in attendance.

However, on one particularly intense anxiety-ridden day, I decided to leave the cafeteria to eat my lunch outside. I found a quiet spot on the grass to sit where I could focus on re-centering myself. A couple of my girlfriends, Michaela and Laurie, spotted me sitting alone and came over to keep me company. Completely unaware of what I was going through internally, they enthusiastically approached me, taking their seats on the grass next to me.

"Hey, Whit. We've come to join you, if that's OK?" Laurie joyfully asked.

Halfway through hearing my friend's voice over the growing anxiety inside my head, I robotically answered, "Yeah, that's fine, sit." Despite being in the expansiveness of outside, I started to feel the world closing in on me. I felt trapped with an overwhelming compulsion to get up and run away. My heart started to pound, joined with the unrelenting, disorienting dizziness that fed the panic. Without warning, I stood up and bolted toward the edge of campus, leaving my friends wondering what the heck had just happened. Driven by adrenaline, I darted across the street, through a small patch of woods, and stopped to catch my breath in the back of an old, rundown Catholic church. Giant pine trees surrounded a neglected cement patio overgrown with weeds and grass, where I found a seat on crumbling stone steps. I reminded myself of what the police officer had told me about finding something to stare at while focusing on my breath. I went through the mental checklist of calming anxiety techniques I had read about in the books in the library.

Slowly inhaling through my nose and out through my mouth, I locked my gaze onto a lone flower growing among the weeds. The dizziness and physical shaking eventually subsided. Once I regained my ground, I glanced up and noticed a massive Great Pyrenees dog sweetly watching me through the church windows. His gentle eyes met mine, and we silently stared at each other for some time. The dog's tail began to wag, and I could see that he was walking toward the back door which led straight to me. I jumped as the door slowly swung open and the sweet beast meandered over toward me. Following the dog came a smiling priest. I quickly stood up, telling him, "I'm so sorry. I'm leaving now."

The priest could tell I was shaken up and kindly replied, "No, no, please, stay. If you don't mind, I'll join you for a few minutes."

I sat back down and watched the tall, husky man slowly stroll over to me. He had a slight limp in his step, and as he walked his dog stayed close by his side, like his guide. He wasn't very old but had the shiniest, most beautiful silver hair that complimented his vestments.

"This is Bruno," the priest told me as he petted the dog's head. Bruno took a seat directly in front of me, allowing me to wrap my arms around his big neck for a hug. "So, would you like to share what's going on? I promise I hold no judgment. It never hurts to have a listening ear," he encouraged me.

I suddenly felt weepy and let the tears stream down my face. With disappointment in my voice, I replied, "I go to the school across the street. I have anxiety and panic attacks. I panicked during lunch, ran off campus, and found myself sitting here."

With softness in his voice, he replied, "Hmm, I understand. We all have our demons to fight. It sounds like you're having a pretty rough day. However, it seems as though you ran to the right place. Bruno is a fantastic friend to hug and talk to when you're feeling a bit lost. He helps me a lot, too."

I wiped the tears from my face and reached out to cuddle Bruno some more. He continued, "Do you want to know a secret of my own? Before I dedicated myself to the Lord, I was very lost. I made decisions and choices that filled me with sorrow and regret. I prayed that someone or something would show me how to take control of my life. Then, one morning at church, a therapist attending the service approached me. He told me to meet him at his office the next day. He felt that God was sending a message to me through him. There were many unresolved resentments and regrets from my past I never dealt with; therefore, creating anxieties and depression for me in the present. The therapist and I prayed together, talked together, and he helped me recognize myself again. This man helped bring me closer to God. The more I surrendered my anxieties to God, the more He freed me of them." The priest's faith in God reminded me of the importance of surrender and trust. He concluded, "The key is to remember you always have a shot at redemption. You are the one in control. It is never too late to change yourself or your surroundings. A hard lesson I've learned over the years is that it's always OK to seek out help."

I smiled at the kind priest as I replied, "It seems as though help sought me out today. Thank you." We sat together for a few moments in silence, Bruno's giant head resting on my lap.

"God works in mysterious ways, doesn't He?" the priest rhetorically asked. I couldn't help but feel as though the universe once again divinely intervened at the exact moment I needed it the most.

Lunch hour at school was quickly coming to an end. As I snuck back onto campus, undetected, a renewed sense of calm cradled me.

PREP SCHOOL (PART 2) & THERAPY

I promised myself I would finish the school year without letting my anxiety get the best of me, but it was beginning to feel seemingly impossible. So, when my mother brought up the idea of finding a therapist, I willingly agreed. I reflected on the priest's story and what he told me about seeking help when it was needed.

My mom booked an appointment with a highly recommended child/family therapist, Dr. Asha (Ph.D. & MD), located in the next town over from where we lived. A few days later, the tiny Indian lady invited me into her office. It smelled of burned sage and sandalwood and was dimly lit in a cozy way. I nervously took a seat in an oversized upholstered armchair positioned across from her. She warmly introduced herself, making me feel welcome and comfortable. She told me she had briefly spoken with my mother over the phone, prior to our meeting but wondered if I could explain why I was seeking her guidance.

I took a deep breath followed by an in-depth look back on the past fifteen years of my anxiety-driven life. The more I talked, the more relaxed I became, and my nervousness disappeared. Vexed and emotionally exhausted by my own story, in a tone of desperation, I asked her, "Do you think you can help me?"

She looked up from the notes she had been jotting down and reassuringly replied, "Anyone who asks for help can be helped. It is a sign you are ready to let go of something and grow."

Immediate relief swept through me.

After a few sessions with my new therapist, she properly diagnosed me with generalized anxiety, social anxiety, and a panic disorder. Because my anxiety was a constant struggle, she recommended that I take medication to help ease the intensity. She prescribed me Zoloft to take each morning before going to school. I was apprehensive about taking prescription drugs but desperate to feel normal so I decided to give it a try.

The next day at school, I arranged a meeting with the student counselor and headmaster. During the lunch hour, the three of us met in the student counselor's office. I was taken by surprise when the headmaster thanked me for initiating the meeting and asked how he could be of assistance. With shakiness in my voice from nerves, I expressed how pernicious and destructive my anxiety had been in all areas of my life, especially my schooling. I told them how I recently learned the term "anxiety" and up until that point had been undiagnosed. Therefore, my anxiety was untreated and out of control. However, I had found and was speaking with a therapist, in addition to trying medication to help the anxiety. Lastly, I told them how I felt my anxiety was stunting my academic performance and that they could expect to see a dramatic improvement on my part. This was a bold statement I was willing to bet on.

"Thank you so much for sharing this with us, Whitney," the headmaster enthusiastically stated. "All of this is such valuable information. With your permission, the first step for us to take is to let all your teachers know what you've been going through and experiencing. The second thing we can do is create an IEP (Individualized Education Program) to support your success as a student."

I was elated by the headmaster's response to me vocalizing my struggles and openly communicating my needs. It was in that moment, I recognized the self-empowerment that came from feeling anxiety and doing it anyway.

Life slowly started to feel more relaxed and enjoyable as I adjusted to weekly therapy sessions, medication, and the personalized support system at school. The more routine and structured my day was, the more I thrived.

More times than not, I would bring my journal into therapy and diligently take notes as Dr. Asha spoke. I asked question after question as if interviewing her. I wanted to understand everything there was to know about anxiety. She patiently welcomed my weekly interrogations as she could see it gave me a sense of control; one of the main objectives for someone in therapy for anxiety disorders. She recognized how I had found writing as a form of self-therapy and encouraged me to utilize it as both a therapeutic and creative outlet. She embraced my love of writing and our sessions became such that she would ask me a "question of the day." I would then spend thirty minutes free-writing my answer, followed by a thirty-minute discussion of what I had written. Her questions always forced me to look within myself for the answers, creating self-reassurance and self-validation. Through writing therapy, I was able to discover I had always searched outwardly for someone to *save me* or tell me I was OK; when in truth, I was the only one who could rescue myself.

As the school year continued and entered into the final quarter, I had fulfilled my promise to the headmaster of noticeably improving my academic performance. I was engaged and able to focus in class, fully present without the distraction of anxiety looming overhead. I was on the honor roll with an "A" average. This was the complete opposite of what I had experienced the previous year in public school. It was as different as night and day. Summer vacation approached and I received a formal invitation back to the prep school for my sophomore year of high school.

09/11/2001

Summer vacation forced an abrupt shift in my daily structure and routine, creating the perfect breeding ground for my anxiety to stealthily creep back in. My family and I traveled to Europe on holiday. When we weren't traveling, my parents were busy working, which made consistent therapy meetings with Dr. Asha difficult. My brain reverted back to the pattern of the anxiety-driven state it had created all those years ago. Although counterintuitive and a bit ironic, living in an anxiety-driven state of mind felt safer and easier than continuing the onerous work of creating a new pattern of non-anxious living. The progress that Dr. Asha and I had accomplished up to that point seemed to be unraveling.

Despite the seemingly obvious choice to go back to prep school that fall, I waffled back and forth on whether or not to return for my sophomore year. The thought of returning to the prep school was daunting and overwhelming. Despite thriving academically, getting through the school year had been laborious and draining. Going back to public school was a menacing and counterproductive prospect. I was holding a double-edged sword. I impulsively made the decision to go back to public school. The same school I had run away from every day two years previously. The same school that depicted me as a "good for nothing, delinquent loser."

Apprehensive about my decision, my father set up a meeting with the headmaster at the prep school, to see if they could hold a place for me in case I changed my mind about retrying public school. We were all completely unaware at the time, but that meeting ended up saving my father's life.

My dad commuted to and from California for business on a regular basis. Like clockwork, he took the same flight every time he flew from Logan Airport in Boston to LAX in Los Angeles. Flight number eleven. He decided to postpone his flight on the morning of September 11, 2001, because the headmaster had scheduled their meeting for the morning of September 12.

I sat in my homeroom class where daily attendance was taken each day. It was one week into the new school year on the morning of September 11, when my good friend, Charlie, burst through the door yelling for the teacher to turn the TV on.

"A fucking plane just flew into one of the twin towers!" There was panic in his voice like I had never heard in anyone before.

The classroom full of chatting students froze in silence. The teacher rushed over to the TV and a terrified news reporter appeared on the screen. Behind her was complete and utter chaos on the streets of New York City. People were running for their lives. Endless sirens of fire engines, ambulances, and police cars blared through the TV.

The news camera scanned upward to film the explosion where the plane had crashed through the building. All of a sudden, the reporter screamed over the chaos, "Oh my God! There's another plane! No! No! Oh my God!"

The camera panned to the right as another plane came into view and crashed into the second twin tower. All of our eyes were glued to the TV. No one moved. No one made a sound. Everyone was in shock at what they were witnessing.

Moments later, the principal's voice came booming through the loudspeaker. "Students and faculty, I just received official notice that the USA is under a terrorist attack. The school day is canceled effective immediately. I would greatly advise each student to go straight home as we are still unsure of any details behind this attack. Please take it upon yourselves to contact your guardians. I repeat, we are under attack. School is canceled effective immediately. May God have mercy on our souls."

An immediate rush of panic strummed through my body. My heart pounded as my trembling hands fished my cellphone from my pocket and dialed my dad. "Collect your things and meet me at the front of the school. I'm coming to get you!" he said, followed by, "Hey, Whit? It's going to be OK."

I frantically grabbed my backpack and bolted for the door.

In a single moment, the safety of my whole world was shattered. Everything suddenly felt so vulnerable, so exposed, so fragile. Something much bigger than myself was in control and all I could do was surrender and pray.

When we got home, my parents, siblings, and I sat around the TV, watching the news in anguish. More information and details about the terrorist attack started to surface. The news anchor tried to hold his emotions together while he was on-air, but tears streamed down his face as he announced the hijacked flights.

"The following flight numbers have been confirmed of the hijacking and terrorist attacks by the Al-Qaeda terrorist organization. American Airlines, flight number 11, Boston to LAX. United Airlines flight number 175, Boston to LAX. American Airlines Flight number 77, Dulles to LAX. United Airlines flight number 93, Newark to SFO." After a long moment of silence on the TV, the man continued, "My unconditional condolences go out to everyone affected by this incomprehensible attack on our nation. God bless you all."

The impact of the day's inconceivable events dug even deeper when my dad spoke, "That was my flight. American Airlines, flight number 11. I was supposed to be on the plane that hit the north tower of the World Trade Center."

We all sat silently on the couch, not knowing how to respond or process the information. The entire day was an emotional overload. We were all eternally grateful to be home, together.

Later that night as I reached for my journal, I couldn't help but break down into tears and weep while I wrote. The events from the day replayed in my head like a broken record. My writing turned into a prayer for all the people who were affected by the awful act of terror.

I lay in bed, listening to the patrolling military jet planes flying overhead every thirty minutes throughout the night. My bed that had been my safe place for so many years didn't feel safe that night. Nothing felt safe. The sun began to rise and I hadn't slept at all. I dragged myself downstairs into the kitchen where my mom was making her morning tea. I turned to her and without hesitation and conviction in my voice stated, "Ma, I'm not going back to school. I quit." Without giving my mom the chance to respond, I turned around and marched back upstairs.

HIGH SCHOOL DROP-OUT

9/11 was my breaking point. The already unstable ground I tip-toed upon had crumbled beneath me. I drew a line in the sand. I was done with school.

My mother got in touch with my therapist right away and scheduled a family therapy session.

Neither of my parents held any understanding or relation to anxiety or panic attacks. They were as new to the term "anxiety" as I was. The difference being they were bystanders witnessing the manifestation of anxiety through me; whereas, I was the one experiencing the mental and physical afflictions of anxiety firsthand. So, I looked forward to sitting down with both of my parents and therapist, with the hope that it would bring my mom and dad some clarity and perspective.

On the day of our family therapy session, I happily walked into my therapist's office, excited to introduce her to my parents. With a warm smile and Indian accent, she introduced herself to my parents. "It is so nice to formally meet the both of you. I am glad we have the opportunity to all sit together and create a team environment not only for Whitney but also for the two of you as her parents."

My father took the lead. "We are all aware of how difficult it has been for Whitney to get through school. After 9/11, she made the decision not to return to high school. I know the terrorist attack affected her deeply. My hope is for you to help Whitney process that trauma, in addition to discussing her dropping out of school."

The excitement of my parents being in the room quickly vanished and anxiety set in when my therapist shifted her focus to me. I sank deeper into my seat, shaking my head "No," a nonverbal signal to her I wasn't ready to speak. With a subtle nod back at me, she responded to my dad's opening statement. "All of your concerns are valid. As parents, you only want the best for your child. When you have multiple children, you become aware that each child has their own needs, independent from one another. Sometimes, you have to adjust your definition of 'what is best' for your children. As hard as you try, you will never fit a square peg into a circular opening. Does this make sense?" My therapist paused for a moment before continuing. "I have been working with Whitney for two years, giving me an in-depth comprehension of who she is and how her anxiety has affected her life. Whitney has an incredibly strong constitution alongside a brilliant mind. I trust her judgment in deciding not to continue school. Perhaps I can ease your tribulations behind this choice."

I sat up a little taller, and a little more confident after hearing my therapist's response.

Knowing she was there to back me up, I turned toward my parents, and bravely stated, "I like to think of myself as a fighter. I also know when to admit defeat. I have painstakingly fought my way through school for as long as I can remember. I am exhausted. I've researched getting my GED (General Educational Development). Not completing high school in the standardized four-year ladder would be a massive stress alleviated from me. It would free up my time, allowing me to focus on getting my anxiety under control with the help of therapy."

Taken aback by both the therapist and my rebuttal, my parents sat quietly for a moment before my father spoke up. "If Whitney decided to pursue getting her GED, would that hinder her getting into college, in the future?"

My therapist reassured my dad. "The GED is the equivalent of a high school diploma. However, instead of going straight from high school to a four-year university, Whitney would go to a community college to obtain her undergraduate degree with the ability to transfer to a university for her graduate degree and higher education."

My dad turned toward me, and with apprehension in his voice, asked, "Are you sure this is what you want?"

I was overflowing with relief, and answered, "Yes, this is what I need."

My parents' fears of their daughter being a high school drop-out were allayed by the help of my therapist. The suffocating grip of the world was loosened from around me enough to take in a deep, relaxing breath. I was grateful.

MOVING FROM MA TO CA

I haven't lived in Massachusetts for seventeen years, but whenever someone asks me where I'm from, my reply is always, Boston. New England runs through my veins and lives in my heart. I love everything about Boston, MA. I love the feisty, no bullshit attitude of Bostonians, the undeviating loyalty and passion for their sports teams, the unmistakable accent (I still have a little bit of mine left), the pride and preservation of the State's history, the multiplicity of cultures and diversity that create the city.

I've lived in and visited states all over the country. None, however, compare to Boston. To me, Boston is always home.

The summer of 2002 brought on a big change. My father's job relocated him to California. My family was leaving Boston, and moving to the suburbs outside Los Angeles. Everything I'd grown up with and knew was about to drastically shift.

The more my house filled with moving boxes, shelves became empty, and the For-Sale sign swung outside on my front lawn, the more the move became real. There was a spark of excitement from the novelty of a cross-country move, a new adventure; but more so an overwhelming sense of sadness and fear of the unknown.

My therapist tried her best to prepare me for the major change that was right around the corner. As we'd discovered a few years previously, I thrived from structure and routine; predictability. Quite the contrary of what was about to happen. Her main concern was keeping my anxiety from spiraling out of control.

A major contributing factor to my anxiety was feeling a lack of control. I had no control over the decision to move, but my therapist helped me identify what I did have control over, including the way I reacted to the coming change. Session after session, we sat together mind-mapping and creating a plan to ease the transition from MA to CA. We wrote everything down so I could refer back to it in moments of anxiety.

I have my therapist's phone number and email address to reach her if needed.

My therapist will help find and refer me to a new therapist in CA.

I have my MA friends' phone numbers to keep in touch with.

I have created a daily routine to stick to every day to reinforce structure and routine.

I own my happiness.

The moving date quickly approached, and the start of formal "goodbyes" to friends, family, and places, created intense emotional turmoil within me. I spent practically every day I wasn't in my therapist's office on the phone with her, as she continuously tried to defuse the ticking time bomb that was my anxiety. On the day of the move, my therapist called to go over the checklist we created together and reminded me to call her later that night to check-in. "You are stronger than you think. You are in control of your anxiety and surroundings. Be brave. You're going to do great in CA." And with that, my journey across the country began.

CROSS-COUNTRY ROAD TRIP

Getting my whole family to California was broken up into three parts. My mom's sister, Barb, helped my mom and I drive across the country with my dog, Brandy. We left four days before my seventeenth birthday. A few days prior to that, my dad and brother had flown together to CA to prepare the house for our arrival. My sister and her boyfriend stayed in MA to tie up loose ends, and then drive cross-country with our other dog, Sky.

It was nearing nightfall when my mom, my aunt, my dog, and myself piled into our Subaru Forester and hit the road.

As my mom slowed to brake at a stop sign at the end of our street, a fleeting thought to jump out of the car and run back home rushed through me. Reality quickly set in, reminding me that my home was now just an empty house. There was no turning back, only moving forward. It was another reminder that change is inevitable, a promised constant in life. And, it was up to me to decide if I was going to fight against it or accept it. "Choose the path of least resistance"—Maharishi Mahesh Yogi.

Sitting in the back seat of the car next to Brandy, I pressed my forehead to the window, looking up at the night sky. Overtaken by a multitude of emotions, I had no option but to embrace the feelings and let them flow through me. As I sobbed staring up at the stars, I prayed that God take my hand and guide me toward contentment.

We were a few days into our cross-country journey and I was losing patience, being stuck in the backseat of the car with Brandy, who refused to sit or lay down the entire trip. Her head stuck out the window, her ass in my face. We were driving through Iowa when I took my turn behind the wheel, a nice break from the backseat. My mom sat in the front passenger seat next to me, my aunt Barb in the back with Brandy. Driving through the rural countryside, we all talked about how we could never live in the Midwest. The landscape was flat and boring, and we were surrounded by endless corn and soy fields. The smell of cow/bull and pig farms was so rank, it was enough to make us nauseous. Little did I know that twelve years from then, I would be living in rural southeast Iowa.

Never having been to the Midwest, we were all clueless as to how intensely fast the weather can shift. I turned my windshield wipers on as the rain started to quickly change from a steady drizzle to a downpour. The drops of rain were so big and loud as they pounded on the car, we had to yell to hear each other. The sky turned an ominous green and dark gray. Lightning started to zap in all directions around us. Huge claps of thunder shook the car. When the rain changed to big balls of hail, my mom said, "This looks like tornado weather. We need to find shelter."

Instant panic set in only to be made worse by my mother yelling at me to "keep my shit together!" while I was driving the car, and my aunt in the backseat praying out loud to Jesus to keep us safe. Fortunately, we came across an underpass to hide beneath while the storm raged around us.

Convinced we were going to be sucked up and torn apart by a tornado, I picked up my cellphone and called my dad. With sheer terror in my voice, I yelled, "We are seconds away from a tornado destroying us! This is the end of the line!"

My mom was yelling that we were NOT going to die, and my aunt was still praying in the backseat when all of a sudden, as fast as the storm came, it dissipated and was gone. The sky turned blue again, the sun was shining, and the only evidence of a storm was a beautiful bright rainbow in front of us.

"Never mind," I told my dad. "We are still alive. But I would appreciate if you bought me a plane ticket. My anxiety can't take finishing this road trip."

The next day was my seventeenth birthday. My mom and aunt dropped me off at the airport in Omaha, Nebraska. I joyfully flew to Los Angeles where my dad and brother picked me up and drove me to our new home to celebrate my birthday.

CULTURE SHOCK
AND EVERYDAY LIFE

My mom and aunt Barb completed the cross-country road trip, arriving four days after me. My aunt stayed for a couple of days to help us settle in before she flew home to MA. Two weeks after that, Heather and Stephen arrived. It was a great comfort having my whole family living together in such a new and different place.

It didn't take much to adjust to the sublime beauty of California. I fell in love with the vast, majestic mountain ranges that surrounded us in all directions, driving through the twists and turns of canyons that lead to the ineffable sight of the Pacific Ocean, and the temperate climate that allowed for year-round hiking, beach-going, or any outdoor activity imaginable.

However, adjusting to the people and their lifestyles was next to impossible for me. The suburb outside Los Angeles where I lived, was home to many celebrities. There was a lot of financial wealth in that town. And with that abundance came a lot of plastic surgery and Botox, high-end designer clothes, expensive foreign cars, multimillion-dollar homes, men with wives twenty years younger than them, and a whole lot of superficialities and materialism I was not used to.

I had just arrived from a place where teenage girls wore sweatpants, Patriots hoodies, Adidas sneakers, threw their hair up in a messy bun, and wore minimal makeup. They looked like actual teenagers. The teenage girls in my new town dressed and acted like they were in their mid-twenties. They walked around in yoga leggings and designer jeans, paired with designer sneakers and high heels, carrying their high-end designer handbags; their hair, makeup, and nails always perfectly manicured. Some already had plastic surgery. It was difficult to relate to and perplexing to witness what defined and validated them; such a tangible contrast from the reality I'd grown up in, in MA.

A few weeks after moving, the new school year started. I was prepared and excited to take the GED test. The test was administered at the community college and was split into two days, with four hours of testing each day. The first day was English and History, and the second day was Science and Math. I had two hours to complete each section. I sat in the classroom, thinking, "Why do people spend four years of their lives going through high school when they could take a four-hour test and be done?"

I passed the test in the 90th percentile, in all four subjects. Obtaining my GED validated leaving high school in the past, and symbolized my growing up.

I was ready to get my first job and was hired as a seasonal Christmas present wrapper at Restoration Hardware. I felt safe being hidden away in the back room, while employees working the sales floor brought gifts to me to be wrapped. It was a really low-pressure job, keeping my anxiety at bay. Once the Christmas season came to an end, so did my employment at the store. My next job was working at a gas station behind the counter as an attendant. The shifts required only one employee to work at a time, so for the most part, with the exception of the occasional manager drop-in, I was on my own. I worked the early morning shift, 4 am-12 pm. The first few hours of work were always dead quiet. This was another low-key, mellow job that didn't affect my anxiety.

Behind the gas station was a shopping center with a Trader Joe's grocery store. One day, someone who worked at the Trader Joe's came in and mentioned that they were hiring, and the starting hourly rate was almost double what I was currently making. Later that day, I walked to Trader Joe's and filled out an application.

A few days later, I received a phone call from Trader Joe's requesting an interview. I excitedly showed up and was hired on the spot. I enthusiastically started my new job, and at first, all was going exceedingly well until my social anxiety started to make its unwelcome re-entrance.

I was still taking the Zoloft prescribed to me a few years earlier by my therapist in MA, Dr. Asha, but I hadn't yet found a therapist in CA to speak with. I reached out to her, and she emailed me a list of therapists in my town that I could connect with. By the grace of God, I found another amazing therapist (Ph.D. and MD) to talk to, Maryjane. She received my records from Dr. Asha and spoke with her over the phone, so she had a relatively good idea of my anxiety before we even started our sessions together.

When I first met Maryjane, I emphasized how my social anxiety was affecting my performance at work. I noticed that the feelings of anxiety I experienced while working were very similar to, if not the same as, what I'd felt while I had been in school. I explained how in the middle of working, seemingly out of nowhere, there would be an overwhelming sense of feeling trapped, followed by an intense impulse to run out and away from work. Also, the anticipation of knowing the next day I had to go back to work would cause debilitating anxiety the night before. I added that when I had been working with Dr. Asha on a weekly basis and did writing therapy, my anxiety was managed much better. I had been able to get my panic attacks, social, and general anxiety under control enough to finish the school year at the prep school. I had come to realize that the symbiotic relationship of weekly therapy and medication was exactly what I needed to thrive and survive.

Maryjane and I picked up where Dr. Asha and I left off. We dove into writing therapy, and she also introduced me to drawing therapy. I would draw my emotions and concerns, then the two of us would look at and dissect the drawing together. She would explain to me what she saw in the picture, and then I would explain what the drawing was trying to convey. Many times, she would point things out I didn't realize I had drawn; deep emotions that my subconscious was releasing. It is a powerful process.

The moment between my therapist and I that will forever be imprinted in my memories, characterizing her as one of my saviors, was the day I opened the conversation about meditation. She had asked me to draw and/or write what my vision of unbounded peace looked like. I drew a picture of myself completely alone, meditating beneath a tree in a snow-covered forest, surrounded by woodland animals. That was the beginning of us integrating meditation into our weekly therapy sessions.

AMMA

My dad learned about Amma from one of his business partners, who kept a photo of Her on his desk in his office. The first time my dad saw the image of Amma, he was compelled to know who She was. His partner explained that She was a Satguru from India who tours the world, spreading the message of unconditional love, compassion, and selfless service.

A few weeks later, right before Thanksgiving 2002, Amma was in Los Angeles on her winter tour. My family decided to go to meet her.

The moment I met Amma, I knew she was my guru. It felt like a reuniting more than an introduction. In that single moment of receiving Amma's Darshan (blessing) for the first time, my entire existence shifted to a whole new reality.

I will forever hold the night I met Amma deep inside my heart. It was the night of Devi Bhava, a special celebration of the divine mother (the Hindu deity, Devi).

A sea of eclectic people awaited her arrival. Some people were long-time devotees, some (like me), had never met Amma before. People of all ages, colors, spiritual, religious, and cultural backgrounds sat side by side, watching the stage in front of them nervously excited with anticipation.

From behind me, a loud conch shell sounded, echoing through the hall, signaling Amma had arrived. Everyone spun around in their chairs to watch the Satguru enter the hall. The moment I saw Amma, the hairs on the back of my neck and arms stood straight up. Electricity was in the air. I watched as she walked through the hall, smiling at everyone she passed and made her way to the middle of the stage to sit cross-legged, closing her eyes in meditation. A sense of complete veneration filled my whole being, I couldn't take my eyes off of Her.

The puja started (an act of worship and respect). Amma blessed holy water with sacred prayer. It was then dispersed among everyone in the hall.

Amma presents her teachings through storytelling. I sat and listened to Her speak, fully engrossed in wonderment. Everything She spoke about, resonated with me on a deep, fundamental level; a way of life I aspired to follow and live by. She talked about living a selfless life; to be of service to others. To have love and compassion for all living beings, and to care for, love, and show respect to our planet.

The puja concluded with a group meditation and prayer of peace for all beings in the world. Amma then stood up and walked behind a curtain on the stage, where she changed into a stunning sari, with a silver jeweled crown atop her head. She channeled and embodied, Devi. The curtains opened and Amma was ready to start giving Her Darshan.

I sat in the crowd, watching Amma embrace people, one by one. Each person received a moment of Her undivided attention and love. Everyone's reaction to receiving Amma's Darshan was their own; some people smiled and laughed blissfully, some people sobbed tears of thanks and reverence, others rendered silent while absorbing the guru's blessing.

When it was my family's turn to go on stage to meet Amma, I was filled with an overwhelming, incomprehensible flood of emotions. It was an out of body experience. My eyes were locked on Amma as we moved our way up the line, closer to Her. My heart pounded, the hair on my body stood straight up again, and shivers rippled up my spine; my body's physical reaction to the puissant energy emanating from Amma.

My dad kneeled down in front of Amma, and then my mom did; Amma hugged my parents as my brother, sister, and myself stood behind them. Amma then gestured for my siblings and me to kneel behind my parents, wrapping our hands around their waists and resting our foreheads against their backs. As a family, we received Her Darshan. When we all stood up to walk off the stage, I felt a tight grasp around my right wrist. I looked down and realized it was Amma holding on to me as my family continued off the stage. Before my brain had a chance to register what was happening, Amma pulled me toward her with a giant smile. For a moment, She and I stared into each other's eyes. Everything around me melted away. It was as if I were staring into the cosmos. She then pulled me close to Her, hugging me and rubbing my back. As I received Amma's hug, it felt as though I was entering into the ether; as if I had left my body and was completely at peace. When Amma pulled me away from Her hug, and our eyes met once again, she smilingly grabbed and pinched both of my cheeks, tossed Her head back as She chuckled, followed by Her sweetly placing Her hand on the side of my face as if to say, "You are finally here. Welcome back."

From that moment on, Amma was my guru. It became my life's work to follow Her teachings and show Her my eternal thanks.

Amma is a living saint. In fact, she is globally known as The Hugging Saint. She has dedicated Her life to philanthropical work and to spreading the message of the power of love. Amma has received countless awards and recognitions for her global charities, selfless acts of kindness, and dedication to helping eliminate darkness from the world.

In December of 2014, Amma sat among a group of other peace-seeking world leaders, including Pope Francis, in the Vatican, where they came together to sign the Interfaith Declaration to end modern slavery. *The Huffington Post* named Amma one of the fifty most powerful female religious leaders in the world.

Amma's project involving global charities is called *Embracing the World*; these charities extend in many directions worldwide, some of which include: Disaster relief after hurricanes, tsunamis, typhoons, floods, and earthquakes. Fighting homelessness by building over 100,000 houses for the homeless. Fighting hunger by serving free meals to the homeless and impoverished in countries all over the world including (but not limited to) the USA, Canada, Africa, India, Europe, Mexico, and Australia. Amma has created orphanages for children in India and Africa, which provide them with education and life skills. AIMS (Amrita Institute of Medical Sciences) hospital in India has provided more than $60 million dollars worth of free medical care, including free pediatric heart surgeries, and eye surgeries reversing or preventing blindness from degenerative eye diseases. And, free physical and dental examinations for those who otherwise couldn't afford healthcare. The Ammachi Labs *Empowering Women* program equips women who are especially economically vulnerable with vocational training and education so they can provide for their families. Amma's volunteers have planted over one million trees worldwide to support the health of the planet. On top of Her inspirational, compelling, endless philanthropy, Amma tirelessly travels the world sharing Her Darshan, and teachings to millions upon millions of people.

To me, Amma is the ultimate example and role model of how to live one's life.

MOVING FROM SoCal TO NorCaL

During the summer of 2007, my father's job transferred him from Southern California (SoCal) to Northern California (NorCal). My parents, Luke, and I moved and lived together, in the suburbs of San Francisco, in the East Bay. Heather and Stephen temporarily stayed in the LA area, before moving north to Santa Cruz, later that year. Leaving SoCal came as a relief since it had been an ongoing struggle for me to relate to the people and lifestyle there. The contrast between NorCal and SoCal was a breath of fresh air. It was a different world.

The people were more down to earth and mellow. There was more culture, and diversity, without the falsities and facades that saturated SoCal living. It carried a New England vibe that reminded me of home. The topography was vastly different, too. We were still surrounded by luscious green mountain ranges, but instead of palm trees and desert, there were giant redwood forests, and the beaches weren't filled with *Bay Watch* wannabes. The transition to the East Bay was made especially easy because the town we moved to had one of Amma's ashrams.

The ashram held weekly Satsangs (a get-together for worship). There were opportunities every weekend to do seva (volunteer work). It was a strong community of Amma devotees, which created a sense of family. The ashram was tucked away in the beautiful, serene, rolling hills, and forest. I would often go there to sit in the stillness and peace of the land that held a reminder of the Divine's omnipresence.

I transferred from Trader Joe's in SoCal to my new town store. It was a comfort knowing I had a job waiting for me when I got there. Having the experience of working for Trader Joe's the past few years made the transition to the new store smooth and easy.

I was speaking with my therapist, Maryjane, over the phone for therapy sessions. I knew I would eventually need to find a new therapist in the East Bay; which was particularly anxiety-evoking because I had built such a close and trusting relationship with her. Much like Dr. Asha, Maryjane provided me with a list of local therapists for me to contact.

The irony was that contacting a new anxiety therapist triggered my anxiety. So, I avoided the process for as long as I could; nevertheless, my anxiety inevitably caught up with me. Before rushing to find a new therapist, I wanted to see how well I could handle my anxiety on my own. Over the years I had acquired many techniques to use during anxiety flare-ups, and I felt confident and prepared to try. It was trial and error, which had its ups and downs, but I was learning that I could rely on myself as my own support system. I felt empowered and strong. Even though what happened next in my life completely blindsided me, it changed my life in ways I never thought possible.

BLESSINGS IN DISGUISE

Augustus 31, 2009. A date that will stay with me forever; the date of my son's conception. A few weeks before I confirmed my pregnancy, Amma came to me in a dream. She was staring into my eyes intensely, as I stared back, getting lost in her boundless eyes. In English, she gently said, "My daughter, you are pregnant. Fear not, for it will all be more than OK." I woke up the next morning feeling freaked out enough about the dream that I told my mother. She shrugged it off telling me, "It's just a dream. Dreams don't necessarily mean anything, Whit."

No matter how much I tried, I couldn't shake the feeling that Amma had come to visit me in that dream.

One month earlier it had been my twenty-third birthday. I had taken a birthday vacation to Boston and apparently had a little too much fun because it was almost October and my period still hadn't made its monthly appearance. So, I went to the store and bought a pregnancy test.

Before giving myself the chance to freak out, I unwrapped the test as fast as I could, popped the cap off, peed on the stick, placed the test on the floor, and left the bathroom. I paced back and forth in my room with a million thoughts racing through my head. "I can't afford a baby! I will be a single mother. I still live at home with my parents. I haven't sorted my life out enough to have a baby. I'm a basket case half the time with my anxiety. How can I take care of a baby when I can't fully take care of myself yet?"

After twenty minutes of freaking out and talking myself down, I went back into the bathroom. When I reached down to pick up the test, I looked the other way and flipped it upside-down so I couldn't see the results. I sat on the edge of the tub, taking a few deep breaths. I thought about throwing the test in the trash without looking at it and pretending as if this wasn't happening. Alas, I knew I needed to know the answer so I could move forward with my life. I counted out loud, "One, two, three," and flipped the test over. The word "PREGNANT" was on the digital screen, clear as day. "Shit!" I yelled. I scrambled to grab the other test from the box. I tore it open, throwing the wrapper and cap on the ground and sat on the toilet. My legs spread wide on either side of the bowl, looking straight down at the test as I peed, the word 'PREGNANT' appeared before I was finished peeing. I dropped the tests in the trash and sat motionless and silent on the toilet, my face buried in my hands.

The thought of Amma and the dream I had, popped into my head. A sense of calm came over me, and tears streamed down my face. "It is all your will," I whispered out loud to Her.

My parents' reaction to my pregnancy wasn't as dreadful as I had anticipated. They trusted the universe and had faith that everything happens for a reason at the time at which it happens. My parents' acceptance of me being pregnant encouraged me to stop worrying about the future and be present with and enjoy my growing belly.

When I was almost four months pregnant, Amma visited the Bay Area ashram during her winter tour. The first night I went to see her, I anxiously awaited my turn to go on stage for Darshan. I wrote on a small piece of scrap paper telling Amma I was pregnant and asking if she could bless my baby.

When I kneeled in front of her, I nervously passed her the scrap of paper, having no idea what to expect. Amma reached out and grabbed the paper from me, and without opening it, held it to her forehead, winked and smiled at me, as if saying, "I already know." She reached to her side and handed me an apple (prasad, blessed food), followed by her rubbing my belly. It was one of the sweetest moments I've experienced with Amma.

As my pregnancy progressed, the more excited I became about becoming a mommy. While I was pregnant, I didn't feel anxiety. It was one of the only times in my life where I didn't experience any sort of anxiety for an extended period of time. I believe it was divine grace keeping my physical body in a calm state while growing my precious baby.

On May 19, 2010, at 12.15 am, I gave birth to the most perfect, beautiful, healthy baby boy. I named him Kaleb Matthew. Kaleb was born with a head full of thick, jet-black hair, giant, round, deep brown eyes, and the most beautiful caramel skin. The moment I met my son, my life changed. I was now living for him. I was improving myself for him. I was his protector, teacher, and best friend, the feeling only a parent understands when they hold their child for the first time. From that moment on, everything I did, every decision I made was for the both of us. It was him and I taking on the whole wide glorious world.

When Kaleb was twelve days old, Amma was back visiting San Ramon during her summer tour. I was bubbling with excitement for Amma to meet my son. For hours, I stood at the bottom right of the stage, rocking Kaleb, watching Amma give Darshan. I wanted to absorb every moment of Amma's presence, and show her thanks for blessing me with the miracle I held in my arms.

When it was my turn to receive Amma's Darshan, I kneeled before Her, holding Kaleb. She reached out with both arms gently taking him from mine. She then looked right at me with Her giant Amma-smile and said, "MY baby!". She snuggled and kissed him all over his precious newborn face before handing him back to me.

I was showered by so much love, so much grace; I was so blessed. I was so grateful.

THE BEGINNING OF THE END

I n June of 2011, during Amma's summer tour, she advised my dad to see a doctor about his health. Her concerned voice carried with it a chilling authority I had never heard from Her before. The instant Her words registered in my consciousness, I knew from the core of my soul, something frighteningly serious was wrong.

My father scheduled a routine physical with his doctor, which quickly spiraled into hospital admissions, endless testing, blood transfusions, and the ultimate diagnosis of colon cancer. A few months following the first cancer diagnosis, a second cancer, separate from the first, was found in one of his kidneys and had spread into his lungs.

At this point, my brother, myself, and Kaleb still lived at home with my parents. Heather and Stephen were engaged and lived in Santa Cruz, CA., two hours away from us. In the midst of my dad's health crisis, my anxiety started spiraling to a place I hadn't known existed. The thought of losing my father sent me into a state of manic panic attacks. My mother temporarily stepped in to help take care of my son, who had just turned one year old.

Day in and day out, my anxiety was wildly out of control. My heart relentlessly pounded out of my chest. I constantly physically shook. I had extreme dry mouth and excessive, unquenchable thirst, and I was spinning-dizzy whenever I stood up. I wasn't sleeping or eating, and eventually, I stopped getting out of bed during the day. I was forced to quit my job because I wasn't functioning.

I had convinced myself that something beyond my anxiety was creating the symptoms I was experiencing. The only time I got out of bed was if I was being driven to the emergency room. Nearly every day, I would go to the ER, convinced that the doctors were overlooking something, and not finding what was wrong with me. The doctors administered every test under the sun, and they would always come back normal. It became increasingly frustrating because I truly felt as though something was wrong with my health, but I wasn't getting any answers. All the times I went to the ER, all the doctors and nurses I came into contact with, not one of them ever mentioned that I was experiencing extreme anxiety and panic; until the day I sat in the office of an endocrinologist.

The doctor was testing my thyroid function. He scrolled through his computer, reviewed my hospital records, and read my symptoms and past test results. He glanced up from his computer and nonchalantly asked, "Have you ever been treated for anxiety? All of your symptoms match extreme anxiety. All your test results are coming back 'normal,' so it is my strong belief that you're experiencing uncontrolled, acute panic attacks."

I told the doctor that anxiety had been a serious, ongoing struggle my whole life, and up until that point, none of the doctors mentioned anxiety as a plausible diagnosis.

Although apprehensive, I followed the doctor's advice to increase the dosage of my Zoloft, and start a new medication, Valium, for panic attacks. He asked me to trust him and give the medication a chance to work. He also referred me to a psychiatrist for continued treatment. It was soon thereafter I met the psychiatrist I credit for saving my life.

DR. HARDY (PART 1)

The day I met Dr. Hardy, my anxiety was so crippling, I could barely walk into her office. She'd received my records from Dr. Asha, and Maryjane, but she didn't know that my dad had just been diagnosed with cancer. I defeatedly slumped down on the couch in her office, with tears in my eyes.

"Whitney, it's really nice to meet you. I've looked over your records and hear you've been having a pretty rough time recently. Why don't you tell me about that?"

This doctor felt warm and kind. She spoke with a comforting softness in her voice, paired with a subtle, yet solid confidence that reassured me that she knew what she was talking about.

With a weeping voice, I told her, "My dad." I looked up at her, frozen, unable to complete my sentence. I took a deep breath and finished, "He has cancer. And it's a really bad kind of cancer. The kind of cancer you can't beat."

We both sat there not saying anything. Dr. Hardy let me be with my feelings for a moment. Before she replied, I added, "I'm a mom. My son just had his first birthday. Kaleb is everything to me. When we found out my dad had cancer, something broke inside me and I completely lost my mind. I convinced myself that I was the one dying. My mom has been helping me take care of my son because I can't function. I need help. I need my life back so I can be a mommy to Kaleb."

Dr. Hardy compassionately smiled at me and said, "First and foremost, you are NOT broken. Your life has just been twisted, turned, and torn apart. You have every right to be losing your shit right now. On top of your dad being sick, you're a new mom. That in itself is a lot. You also have an intense anxiety and panic disorder that makes everything way more intense. I promise you, we will grab your anxiety by the reins and regain your control."

I breathed a heavy sigh of relief. For the first time in weeks, I felt a glimmer of ease.

Dr. Hardy shared with me that she'd lost her mother to cancer during her first pregnancy. Hearing her story created an instant, profound trust, and bond between us. I was assuaged knowing I wasn't alone with the debilitating feelings that came with losing a parent to such a harrowing disease.

She gave me her personal cellphone number to call in case I needed to get in touch with her in-between sessions. She carved out hour-long appointments with me from her schedule, which otherwise would be twenty minutes. She went above and beyond to help me feel safe and supported.

Within a few days of taking the increased dose of medication, I noticed the intense physical symptoms of anxiety and panic begin to calm down and subside. I was able to sleep through the night and get out of bed in the mornings with Kaleb. My appetite came back, allowing me to fuel my body with nutrients and energy. In turn, I felt more in control and balanced within myself. It was the tip of the iceberg, but I was ready to dive headfirst into the depths of my anxiety, to get my life back.

CAREGIVER

Watching my dad slowly and painfully wither away from cancer and chemotherapy was one of the hardest things I've witnessed. My dad had always been so strong and impenetrable, but all of a sudden, he was frail, weak, and vulnerable.

I stayed home with Kaleb and my dad during the day, and my mom went back to work, in retail, full-time. I took over being my dad's caregiver. Helping my dad brought me a sense of peace about him being so sick. It brought us closer together and enabled him to spend time with his only grandchild.

While Kaleb and I would wake up and make ourselves breakfast each morning, I'd have my phone nearby, waiting for my dad to text me that he was awake. Kaleb and I would go upstairs and start the taxing process of helping my dad out of bed, and to get ready for the day. Most days, it was a grueling two-hour process.

We had our routine down like clockwork. He'd slowly, and painfully sit his stiffened body up, dangling his legs off the side of the bed. I stood next to him, his medicine pillbox and a glass of water in hand. He would reach his hand out, signaling he was ready for his first pill. He was very specific about the order in which he took his medication, and I had it memorized. The only pill I could never touch was his chemotherapy one; it was too toxic.

Next, it was time to stand him up. I would hold out my forearms like railings for him to grab onto. He had become too weak and frail to pull himself up on his own, so I would have to lean my body weight backward, countering his weight, and pull him to his feet. I'd link arms with him and baby-step toward the bathroom.

"Hi, baby," my dad would say, looking down at Kaleb patiently playing with his favorite Hot Wheels cars. "Hi, Papa!" Kaleb always enthusiastically greeted him. They brought each other so much joy.

Once we made it to the bathroom, it was time to get him in the shower. He would undress himself and wrap a towel around his body while I turned the water on and adjusted the temperature. I'd wait outside the shower, ready to hand him his towel. He'd always go inside his walk-in closet and put his boxers and shirt on, for a bit of privacy. We would then baby-step back to his bed where he could balance on the edge of the mattress to get his pants and socks on.

My dad would stay balanced on the edge of the bed while I collected everything he needed to get him downstairs; his medication, laptop, books, an extra sweater, and his glasses case. Kaleb was so used to the routine, that when he saw me getting my dad's belongings together, he would pick up his hot wheels and wait for me at the top of the stairs. I would walk Kaleb downstairs first, place my dad's things down on the dining room table, and run back upstairs to help him slowly, and carefully descend the stairs.

We would walk together, arms linked, to the couch. I would prop the pillows behind and around him, creating a support-nest, hand him the TV remote, and his things I'd brought downstairs. He would decide what he wanted for breakfast, and I would prepare it for him. Kaleb always liked climbing up next to my dad on the couch while he ate his breakfast. It was their quality time together.

I cherished every moment I had with my father. It illuminated my heart full of joy, watching my son and dad create such a powerful, steadfast bond. Kaleb gave my dad something to keep fighting and living for.

Kaleb and I would play outside in our backyard or walk to the park across the street, always ready to run home if my dad texted me. I was always on call. I made sure I was home to make my dad lunch and check that he was OK.

It was tricky finding a balance of being available and present with my dad as his caregiver and being available and present with Kaleb as his mommy. It was never a burden, more so exhausting. It was always a relief when my mom got home from work and took over caregiving for my dad at night.

DR. HARDY (PART 2)

Being a full-time single mom and taking care of my dad was no simple task. It was easy to forget to take care of myself. Dr. Hardy helped me to stay present in the moment, and acknowledge and process my feelings and emotions. She didn't want me to mentally check out, suppress, or avoid what I was experiencing. Otherwise, it would eventually boil over into another unwelcome mental breakdown.

My sessions with Dr. Hardy were as precious as gold. They were my one hour of me-time. We dove into writing therapy, which helped bring up and release painful emotions I didn't have time to think about during the day while I was with Kaleb and my dad. We also integrated meditation into my therapy as a form of relaxation after discussing deep and difficult emotions.

Although we had my panic attacks under control, for the most part, my general and social anxiety still onerously dictated my everyday life. The mere thought of leaving the house triggered great anxiety. Dr. Hardy told me this was called agoraphobia. The less I left the house, and hid inside, the more the phobia grew bigger and scarier. She knew I had no choice but to leave the house to bring my dad to doctor's appointments, and run errands, which worked to an advantage in the situation; helping to break the agoraphobic cycle.

She and I created a daily routine for me to stick to every single day, without fail. I wrote the routine in my notebook, starting from the moment I woke up, hour by hour, step by step. I decided I would start waking up an hour before Kaleb to meditate and gently welcome the new day. Dr. Hardy suggested I add daily walks into my routine. It would double as an anxiety release and would be good practice leaving the house on my own. I took the routine we created very seriously. I was determined to do whatever it took to break the vicious cycle of anxiety.

Every day I would put Kaleb in his stroller and walk across the street to the park. There was a paved path that circled around the park, perfect for walking. It didn't take long for me to start to feel the benefits of walking every day. I had more energy, and if I was having a rough day, walking would help alleviate the suffocating grip of anxiety. It got both Kaleb and me out of the house and into the fresh air.

One day, while Kaleb and I played at the park after my walk, I had the thought to try jogging the next time instead of walking. I didn't know it at the time, but that one thought would eventually bring me to crossing the San Francisco Rock 'n' Roll Marathon finish line.

LEARNING TO RUN

I'm the type of person who gets an idea in my head, creates a plan, and executes. Much like anything someone wants to become good at, they have to practice; and, jogging is no exception to that rule. My love for studying came into play, and I researched the process of both physical and mental training to teach my body how to run. I read autobiographies about people's personal journeys of running and watched countless YouTube videos on how to build endurance and stamina; and, how to train my breath while jogging. I created a log that tracked my weekly progress. Next, it was time to put my plan into action.

With Kaleb in the jogging stroller, I would walk over to the park to practice. I started off slowly, alternating between walking and jogging a quarter-mile at a time. I inched my way up in distance, eventually eliminating the alternation of walking and jogging, and was able to steadily jog without needing a break. Later, I graduated from the small circles around the park, to jogging around the neighborhood and town.

It was invigorating to feel my heart race and adrenaline pump in a positive, encouraging way. It didn't take long for me to recognize the physical, mental and therapeutic benefits of jogging. It was a great release from the stress of taking care of my dad, and created an extra hour of me-time during the day. For me, jogging was a tangible letting go of, and leaving the past behind with each stride forward.

One morning, while sitting on the couch with Kaleb and my dad, I got an email on my phone from one of my friends. She had forwarded me the register for the San Francisco Rock 'n' Roll Marathon, and half-jokingly said that she and I should register for the race. I absentmindedly read the email out loud, and was surprised to hear my dad ask, "So, are you going to do it?" I looked at my dad without saying anything, and he continued, "You can do it. No regrets! Go big or go home! Kaleb and I will wait for you at the finish line." His smile and belief in me had me determined to run that race.

At the time, it was October 2013, and the marathon was in April 2014. I had six months to train for the race.

JANUARY 2, 2014

I t was nearing Christmas, and my grandma Selma, my dad's mom, came from New York to celebrate the holidays. My dad hadn't seen his mother for a few years so he was especially excited. It was the first time she was going to meet Kaleb.

She was a skinny, old, Jewish lady, in her late eighties, from The Bronx, NY, and blind as a bat. She arrived at our house on December 22nd. I knew it was going to be an extra person to take care of, so I planned our days leading up to Christmas to be mellow. I continued with my daily routine, adding in my grandma.

I looked forward to my me-time, leaving the house for an hour with Kaleb to jog. I was grateful for every minute we had alone. It was not an easy job caring for my toddler, my sick father, and my old, blind grandma. Going for my jog was my reset button. It expelled all of my pent-up anxiety and stress, and I was outside breathing fresh air, finding my center.

On December 23, my dad called to me as I was in the kitchen making everyone breakfast. He had made his way downstairs and into his office, where I was surprised to find him standing and holding my favorite photo of a flower he had taken. He looked at me in a way he never had before, and asked, "Do you want to keep this image?" Without answering him I asked, "Why are you giving this away to me?"

He paused, looking at me softly in my eyes, and without answering, he asked, "Can you get Kaleb and bring him in here?"

My guts turned as I walked away from him to get Kaleb. When Kaleb stepped into his office, my dad was holding an antique windup toy robot that had always sat on my dad's desk. Kaleb never understood why my dad had a toy on his desk he never played with. "Hi, baby," my dad greeted Kaleb. "Hi, Papa!" Kaleb looked up at my dad with his giant brown eyes. "Would you like to keep this robot?" my dad asked, handing him the toy. "Ok!" Kaleb joyfully answered.

"You promise you'll take really special care of this toy?" my dad asked.

"Yes! I will be so careful!" Kaleb innocently replied and then turned to walk out of the office and show my grandma his new toy.

"Dad, why are you giving away your things?" I asked, tears rolling down my cheeks.

My dad just looked at me with a half-smile and said, "Let's go upstairs and get me dressed so we can all have that breakfast you made, eh?"

I wasn't going to force my dad to say anything he obviously wasn't ready to say, so I wiped my eyes, took a deep breath and walked him upstairs.

While I helped my dad put on his socks, I couldn't hold back my tears.

"Hey," he said, "What's going on, Whit?"

Everything I had been holding inside for the past two-and-half years came pouring out of me. I cried so hard that I lost my breath. My dad sat next to me, his arm around my shoulder, tight.

"I'm just sad. I'm sad for you. I'm sad that you're in so much pain. You must be exhausted. Don't you ever feel defeated? Don't you ever want to just give up and not have to hurt anymore?"

My dad cut me off from my meltdown by saying, "You don't EVER give up on life. Life may knock you down and give up on you, but *you* don't EVER give up on life. You always keep fighting. You promise me something, OK? Whatever happens, you keep moving forward. No looking back, no regrets, just moving forward."

My dad's word was his bond. If he promised something, he meant it. If he asked you to make a promise, he expected you to uphold that promise. I looked my dad in his eyes and promised him that no matter what happened, I would always keep moving forward. We squeezed each other tight for a moment before linking arms to walk downstairs to eat breakfast with Kaleb and my grandma.

On Christmas morning, Kaleb woke up early and excited. My grandma joined us as I made our usual morning coffee, and waited for my mom, dad, and Luke to make their way downstairs. Kaleb was becoming restless waiting to open his presents, so I went upstairs to check on my parents.

I knocked on their door, and quietly opened it, saying, "Merry Christmas!" I froze in my tracks when I saw my dad lying in bed, white as a ghost and with his lips blue, unable to move. My mom told me she had called an ambulance and they were already on their way. I ran to the side of my dad's bed and grabbed his hand. It was stiff and cold. "Dad! What's going on? Are you ok?" I felt sick to my stomach. He looked up at me, and I could tell it was difficult for him to talk.

He quietly said, "Make sure Kaleb and my mom have a good Christmas, OK?"

My heart sunk to the floor as I replied, "Ok, I promise." I kissed his forehead and then ran into Luke's room to wake him up, and tell him what was happening. I then went downstairs to let my grandma know. As I sat next to her on the couch, we could hear the sirens in the distance getting closer to our house. I squeezed my grandma tight, and we sat together as Kaleb opened his presents.

The medics arrived and quickly carried my dad down the stairs and out to the ambulance. I had promised my dad to show Kaleb and my grandma a good Christmas so

I swallowed the frantic desire to jump in the car with my mom and chase the ambulance to the hospital. My grandma and Luke, who I'm sure were both freaking out inside, did a good job helping me give Kaleb a good Christmas morning.

Heather and Stephen arrived an hour later, and we all anxiously waited to hear from my mom. My phone rang and to my surprise it was my dad, FaceTiming me. I held the phone up so he could see everyone.

"Hi, guys, Merry Christmas," he said, smiling. He looked much better than when he had left the house earlier. "The doctor said I have an infection in my intestines, and they need to operate to clear it all out. They will do it first thing tomorrow morning. Everything is going to be just fine. Try to enjoy your Christmas."

Later that night, Kaleb and I FaceTimed my dad before we went to bed.

"Papa? I love you, Papa. Come home soon so we can play and you can watch baseball on the couch with me, OK?" Kaleb kissed my dad through the phone.

"I will, baby. I'll be home really soon. I love you too." My dad kissed Kaleb through the phone. I looked at my dad through the little screen, and everything in me told me to memorize his smile. "I love you, Dad. I'll see you soon."

He smiled, "I love you too, Whit. Goodnight."

The next morning, my mom left before sunlight to be with my dad at the hospital during his operation. I was up at the crack of dawn to help my grandma get into the taxi that would drive her to the airport so as to fly back to New

York. I promised her that I would keep her updated every time I heard anything from my mom. She didn't have to say much for me to feel her sorrow and grief. I kissed my grandma's cheek, gave her a big squeeze, and helped her into the taxi.

The morning hours passed by painfully slow. When the morning turned into afternoon and I hadn't heard anything from Mom, I started to get worried. Finally, she called and said that there was far more infection than the doctors had originally thought, so the operation had taken much longer than anticipated. Also, my dad's intestines were too swollen from the infection to be put back inside of him and stitched up. They would bandage and cover his intestines, and keep him sedated to give the swelling a chance to go down. Only then could they finish the operation.

The next few days turned into a painstaking waiting game, praying for the swelling of his intestines to go down enough to finish the operation. The longer he was sedated, the more brain function my dad lost. It was a slippery slope.

I called a close friend, Sudha, who helped coordinate one of Amma's senior disciples, Swami Dayamrita, to come to the hospital and pray over my dad. It was such a tender, selfless, moment I will always hold close to my heart. I know that was what my dad would have wanted.

My dad's operation was on December 26, and by the 31st, the swelling of his intestines wasn't going down, and his body was getting weaker every day. The doctors were worried that he wouldn't make it through surgery even if his intestinal swelling went down enough to finish the operation.

The moment came where we had to choose between chancing my dad's life on the operating table, and quality of life afterward if he made it through the surgery, or, taking him off life-support and letting him pass away surrounded by his family. We chose the latter. We arranged for the date of January 2, 2014.

On New Year's Eve night, my mom and I stayed at the hospital with my dad. My brother offered to stay home with Kaleb. My mom and I prayed over my dad and talked to him. "Happy New Year, Daddy. I'll be sleeping right next to you, OK?" I pulled my chair up next to his big hospital bed, gently took his hand, and fell asleep.

The next morning, I went home to Kaleb, and my brother went to visit my dad. Later, when my mom came home to shower and rest, she stayed home with Kaleb, and I went back to the hospital to sit with my dad. We worked as a team, rotating shifts from home to the hospital and back again. My brother offered to stay home with Kaleb again, so my mom and I stayed overnight with my dad. I sat awake, next to my dad, unable to sleep. I knew what the morning would bring. There was no fighting time. All I could do was surrender to God's will, and pray over my dad.

Early the next morning, my friend Sudha arrived at my house to look after Kaleb while my brother met my mom and me at the hospital. The three of us quietly waited for Heather and Stephen to get there. There wasn't much to say. We were all internalizing the moment, and praying for my dad. Shortly after Heather and Stephen's arrival, my dad's nurse came into the room. She turned down the dial of my dad's sedative and yelled to him, "Barry! Can you hear me, honey?"

My dad subtly nodded his head, "Yes."

"Your family is here to see you, Barry."

Again, he nodded his head, "Yes."

The nurse turned toward all of us and explained the process of taking my dad off life-support. We all took a moment to breathe a few deep breaths and told the nurse we were ready.

"Barry, we're going to take your tube out, OK?" The nurse yelled, standing next to my dad. My dad, for the last time, nodded his head, "Yes."

"One, two, three," the nurse counted out loud, pulling the long tube up and out from my dad's throat.

We were all motionless as we watched my dad force his eyes open to look at all of us one last time.

The nurse left the room and let us be with him in his final moments. My mom sat next to my dad on the left side of the bed, holding his hand. I sat on the right side of the bed holding his other hand. Luke stood behind the right side of the bed, gently touching my dad's head. Heather sat at the end of the bed being comforted by Stephen. I placed my head on my dad's chest, selfishly holding on to every heartbeat I could. Every beat grew fainter and quieter until it eventually stopped. I looked up at my mom and whimpered, "He's gone."

We all sat in silence, paying our deepest respects to my daddy. He surrendered to the Lord and was now resting in the arms of the divine.

SAYING GOODBYE

My mom reached out to extended family and organized a memorial service for my dad. My aunt Barb, aunt Ruthie, aunt Kathy, my mom and aunt's cousin, Cath, and my dad's best friend, Neil, all flew out from the east coast for my dad's service. My mom, Heather, Stephen, Luke, Kaleb, and I all met at the ashram where the service was held.

We wrapped my dad's ashes in a beautiful silk scarf and placed them down on a wooden meditation structure. We stood in the grass-covered field for a few moments of silence. My mom stepped forward and briefly said her goodbyes to my dad. She asked if anyone else wanted to say anything about my father. I waited for my brother, sister, or Stephen to step forward and say something, but no one did.

So, I walked up and stood next to my dad's ashes. Standing next to his ashes felt just the same as if he were in his human body, standing next to me. It gave me strength, courage, and a sense of calm, as I looked at my family and began to read the eulogy I had written for my dad. I was proud to stand before my dad's ashes, and represent who he was, and all he had gone through. My dad was a warrior, and it was my honor to have been by his side when he needed it the most.

I finished my tribute with the words my dad had told me a few days before he went to the hospital, "Whatever happens, keep moving forward. No looking back, no regrets, just moving forward."

We took some of his ashes and scattered them under the trees that grew all around the field where we stood. I walked Kaleb down to the pond and asked if he wanted to scatter some of his Papa's ashes into the water.

"This is Papa? Inside this box?"

I kneeled by Kaleb's side and I answered, "Yes, baby. Papa is in this box, and we're returning him to nature."

Kaleb looked inside the box for a moment, and I could see him trying to figure out why my dad was ashes. His little hand reached into the box and scooped out a fist full of ashes. He reached his arm back and threw the ashes into the pond yelling, "Go, Papa! Go to Amma! Be free, Papa! Be Free!" We stood at the water's edge for a minute, watching the ashes sink and float away with ripples of water. "Bye-Bye, Papa," Kaleb said before he turned around, ready to leave. As I turned to follow my son, a gust of wind blew through the field carrying with it a sense of electricity. Goosebumps covered my body, and my heart skipped a beat. I looked up at the cloud-covered sky, and told my dad, "I knew you were here. Thank you, Daddy."

DR. HARDY (PART 3) AND ROCK 'N' ROLL MARATHON

Dr. Hardy was an incredible support system for me after my father's passing. I knew she understood the feelings, emotions, and grief that came with losing a parent.

We did a lot of writing and meditation therapy together to process some of my grief. Some days, I needed to talk the whole time, and vent it out of my system. Other days, I needed to sit and cry. Dr. Hardy let me lead the way through the passage of grief, and was there as a compassionate hand to hold, and shoulder to cry on.

The marathon I was training for was in April. My father wasn't able to wait at the finish line for me anymore; however, I was determined to run the race in his honor. Dr. Hardy agreed that training for the race would be a good and continuous way to release anxiety and grief; something to keep focused on and look forward to in the near future. She knew running the marathon would be very cathartic, and a sweet way to honor my dad. She was a great supporter of my training.

April 6, 2014, was race day. I woke up at 3.30 am and drove to San Francisco. There I climbed into one of the many buses lined up, waiting to drive all the runners to the start-line. As everyone unloaded from the buses and found their starting corrals, I took a few minutes to mentally prepare myself for the race. I unzipped my fanny pack and carefully took out the small bag of my dad's ashes I had placed there earlier that morning. I held his ashes to my heart, closed my eyes, and spoke out loud to him. "Dad, please run this race by my side. Fuel me with the mental and physical strength to finish this race. I know you're here with me." I kissed the bag and zipped it back into my fanny pack.

The announcer's voice enthusiastically boomed over the loudspeaker. "Gooooood morning, San Francisco! Are you ready to ROCK N' ROLL?"

He was getting the runners pumped up and excited to race.

"Here we go! Three! Two! One!" The starter gunshot sounded through the speakers, and the race began.

"Come on, Dad, let's run," I told him, as I took my first of many strides.

As I ran up and down the rolling San Francisco streets, past the beautiful, old Victorian homes, and alongside the shoreline of the beach, I couldn't help but feel so grateful for every breath I took. It was indescribably exhilarating to run across the Golden Gate Bridge. Everyone cheered for and supported one another. The collective energy of thousands of people running together toward the finish line was incredibly powerful.

About halfway through the run, exhaustion set in and my body went into auto-pilot mode. My legs were moving but I felt disconnected from my body. I supposed that was what a runner's high felt like. Mile after mile, I trekked on.

Just when I'd started to think my body might give out, I rounded a corner and saw a giant hilly street in front of me. "You have got to be kidding me. Just keep moving forward," I whispered to myself, as my speed slowly started to decrease up the hill.

"Just think of the downhill jog you'll enjoy in just a few minutes!" a passing runner smilingly encouraged me.

One foot in front of the other, I finally made it to the top. Not only was there a giant downhill run waiting for me, but so was the finish line.

I reached into my fanny pack and pulled out my dad's ashes. I kissed them and held them toward the sky. "We did it, Dad! We did it!" I zipped the ashes back into my fanny pack and started to sprint to the finish line. As I gained speed down the hill, I heard someone yell, "Fuck yeah, Whit! You got this!" I looked over to see my sister and brother-in-law cheering me on. My heart filled with love from their support as I raced down the hill and crossed the finish line.

I found Heather and Stephen looking for me on the rest-field where people sat to recuperate after the run. They gave me a big hug and said congratulations. I could do nothing more than lie down on the grass, stare up at the sky, and be grateful.

MOVING TO IOWA

When my dad passed away, there was a financial shift for us as a family. My mom and I exhausted our search in trying to find an affordable place to live in California.

A long-time friend of my parents, Sheila, from the TM community, reached out to my mom, encouraging us to move to Fairfield, Iowa. Fairfield was the central hub of the TM movement. She expressed how strong and close-knit the small community was, and how healing and supportive it would be to live there. In addition, the cost of living made life easy.

I was reluctant to even consider the idea of moving to Iowa. Remembering the cross-country road trip in 2002 when we'd driven through the flat, boring, endless cornfields of Iowa, was enough to turn me off from ever wanting to live there. The thought of leaving the ashram, and the Amma community behind, broke my heart. And, the thought of leaving Dr. Hardy was terribly frightening.

However, I knew my mom had been through so much already with losing her husband, and now having no choice but to move out of state, away from her other children. So, I didn't argue when she leaned toward moving to Iowa.

In June 2014, we packed the U-Haul truck, kissed California goodbye, and headed to the Midwest. There was a lot of adjusting and getting used to with small-town, country living. Fairfield has a population of nine thousand people and is 6.4 square miles. Downtown was lined with "mom and pop" stores, no mainstream businesses. It was normal to see tractors driving down the road next to cars. It was easy to get lost on the long, winding, gravel, country roads that wrapped through corn and soy fields. And, on windy days, the air was saturated with the stench of hog farms. Quite a palpable difference from where we'd lived on the west coast. It took me a few years, but I slowly started to enjoy the slow, laidback, Midwestern way of living.

Dr. Hardy was able to continue therapy with me for six months before I would legally have to find a local therapist. We spoke on the phone twice a week for sessions, and I was able to call or email her in-between sessions if needed. I found a local psychiatrist to help with my medication management and spoke with Dr. Hardy for as long as I could. She helped me adjust to moving to Iowa, creating an everyday routine for myself and Kaleb, and worked with me through the grieving process of losing my dad.

Six months flew by and my time with Dr. Hardy was coming to an end. She reassured me that I could always email her whenever I needed. She told me to save her phone number in case I ever needed to call. I was nervous and sad to stop my sessions with her. She'd helped me through some of the most difficult moments of my life. I told myself, "As one door closes, another one opens." I was experiencing another moment where I needed to surrender and trust the support of nature. I was completely unaware at the time, that my next therapist would help change my life forever.

BREAKING UP WITH ANXIETY

The first day I met Scott, I learned he was a "no bullshit" kind of guy. He was all about getting to the point and finding a solution. Scott had his own unique approach to therapy. It was integrative, which meant that he used multiple therapy techniques that he individualized specifically for each of his patients.

Scott's motto is to always "Take action!" He teaches and reinforces that anyone is capable of retraining and reconstructing their brain to its optimal functionality.

When I first met Scott, I was in an emotionally vulnerable place, and I was sick and tired of my anxiety always flaring up and debilitating my life. I walked into his office with frustration in my voice and tears in my eyes. I told him I felt defeated by my anxiety.

"I get that you *feel* frustrated, you *feel* defeated, you *feel* sad. I'm not taking those feelings away from you. I'm not saying those feelings aren't real. What I'm asking you is, what are you going to *do* with those feelings? What are you going to create from them?"

I looked at Scott, confused, not knowing what to say because all the answers I could come up with had the word "feeling" in them.

He rephrased his question. "Everything is a decision. What is your decision?"

I paused, looked at him square in the eyes, and replied, "I'm breaking up with anxiety."

"Yes!" he exclaimed. "Understand that you are in control."

And so, commenced my journey to break up with anxiety.

Scott's approach to therapy switched my thinking from being a victim of anxiety to knowing I am the one in control of my anxiety.

Over the years, Scott has "kicked me in the ass" more than a few times, showing me tough love, like a reality check. I'm what's considered "a runner." I will run away from my anxiety, not wanting to face it. I shove it down and away, hoping it will magically disappear. But it always comes back to haunt me. Scott doesn't allow me to run away anymore. Now, I run toward the anxiety. Truly understanding that I am in control of my anxiety breaks away the fear of facing it, dealing with it, and releasing it from my body.

The moment I started to hold myself accountable for my own anxiety and chose to be present and in control of it, I saw a quantifiable shift in my life. I am able to be a full-time single mom to my amazing son, work full-time from my home, and continue working on creating the best version of myself.

The universe aligned me with each therapist I've worked with over the years at the exact moment in time I needed them; to build trusting, healing, and supportive bonds in the exact way I needed them at the time. It is cumulative effort over the years of determination, courage, self-love, therapy, and the support of nature, which makes taking control of anxiety possible. Instead of separating my anxiety from my happiness, I marry them together and smile through it. It's a forever journey that may be a part of me but does not define me.

"Whatever happens, keep moving forward. Always move forward."—Barry W. Bomzer 10/31/1949–01/02/2014.

Made in the USA
Columbia, SC
12 December 2020